T0013299

DREAMTIMES
AND
THOUGHTFORMS

"Grossinger hurls his mastery of esoteric wisdom, a profound understanding of the cosmos, and his exquisite poetic expression at the reader like the bright light of an asteroid whizzing past Earth's orbit. A breathtaking read!"

PATRICIA CORI, AUTHOR, SCREENWRITER,
AND FORMER HOST OF BEYOND THE MATRIX

"We live in a wild cosmos, a multidimensional multiverse teeming with all sorts of intelligences and mysteries. *Dreamtimes and Thoughtforms* is an invitation into a bigger cosmological story that makes room for all the beauty and paradox we are enveloped in by (in)visible worlds. In these pages, Grossinger performs his trademark meta-integration magic—weaving together animal intelligence, UFOs, ghosts, and esoteric cosmologies into a wonderfully wild song of ourselves and the worlds around us, containing multitudes."

SEAN ESBJÖRN-HARGENS, PH.D., DEAN OF INTEGRAL EDUCATION
AT CALIFORNIA INSTITUTE FOR HUMAN SCIENCE AND
COEDITOR OF *METATHEORY FOR THE ANTHROPOCENE*

"*Dreamtimes and Thoughtforms* examines the inner and external landscapes of consciousness. Exploring the primordial universe and/or multiverse, primitive biological life, physics, psi, dreams, philosophy, anthropology, and ancient writings, Grossinger goes beyond surface-level discussions and embraces deep contemplation and open-mindedness. Recognizing that consciousness is the builder of all we experience, the author realizes that one may survey the greater reality more effectively through inner vision than a set of eyes. When looking out to observe the external world, we, in some way, see a reflection of ourselves."

MARK IRELAND, AUTHOR OF *SOUL SHIFT*

"*Dreamtimes and Thoughtforms* takes forward, with new inputs, the project Alfred Jarry undertook in his Faustroll writings at the end of the nineteenth century. Like Jarry, Grossinger reads science through an esoteric lens and esoteric thinking through the lens of science, thus enriching our sensibilities, unmooring our imaginations. In his own terminology, perhaps Jarry was a preincarnation of Grossinger."

FRED D'AGOSTINO, PH.D., RETIRED PROFESSOR OF
HUMANITIES AT THE UNIVERSITY OF QUEENSLAND

"From the Big Bang to bacteria to the microbiomes, the Cambrian explosion, and catastrophic events, Richard Grossinger outlines the universe and the limitations of materialistic science in explaining 'all that is,' for there is more to life than math, chemistry, and physics. A great read; highly recommended."

JOHN A. RUSH, PH.D., N.D., AUTHOR OF
JESUS, MUSHROOMS, AND THE ORIGIN OF CHRISTIANITY

"In *Dreamtimes and Thoughtforms*, the reader will learn about the spiritual concepts that date back to the Big Bang and how they relate to reincarnation, past-life memories, ghosts, and even to the intelligence of crows and octopuses. This is a sensational investigation into how beliefs and thoughtforms create reality."

DAVID BARRETO, AUTHOR OF
SPIRITUAL EVOLUTION IN THE ANIMAL KINGDOM

"Like his masterpiece *Deep Pool of Light*, the meanings flow from the pages to our souls, creating a new language of the sacred. Richard's work is best seen perhaps as the scripture of an expanding cosmos written for a distant age beyond our present vision. It's as though he can observe and celebrate from a distant galaxy our own Milky Way, nucleus to nova, or slide down a cosmic wormhole and document the journey!"

ALBERT J. LaCHANCE, AUTHOR OF *CULTURAL ADDICTION*
AND COAUTHOR OF *THE THIRD COVENANT*

"When I read Richard's words I am uplifted and encouraged to fully envelop my mind in the psychospiritual, metaphysical spaces he makes so accessible. *Dreamtimes and Thoughtforms* is a profound treatise on the vanguard of how we cognize and ingest the super mundane and come to know the full expression of the living cosmos, all around and within."

JOSHUA REICHMANN, FILMMAKER AND MUSICIAN

"Reminds me of a Bob Dylan song."

JOHN FRIEDLANDER, AUTHOR OF *RECENTERING SETH*

DREAMTIMES
AND
THOUGHTFORMS

Cosmogenesis from the Big Bang
to Octopus and Crow Intelligence to UFOs

RICHARD GROSSINGER

Park Street Press
Rochester, Vermont

Park Street Press
One Park Street
Rochester, Vermont 05767
www.ParkStPress.com

Text stock is SFI certified

Park Street Press is a division of Inner Traditions International

Cataloging-in-Publication Data for this title is available from the Library of Congress

ISBN 978-1-64411-564-0 (print)
ISBN 978-1-64411-565-7 (ebook)

Printed and bound in the United States by Lake Book Manufacturing, Inc. The text stock is SFI certified. The Sustainable Forestry Initiative® program promotes sustainable forest management.

10 9 8 7 6 5 4 3 2 1

Text design and layout by Debbie Glogover
This book was typeset in Garamond Premier Pro with Adobe Jenson Pro, Antonio, Gill Sans MT Pro, and ITC Legacy Sans Std used as display typefaces

To send correspondence to the author of this book, mail a first-class letter to the author c/o Inner Traditions • Bear & Company, One Park Street, Rochester, VT 05767, and we will forward the communication, or contact the author directly at **www.richardgrossinger.com**.

For Sean Murphy, Andrew Hasse, Sarah Scheld,
Ash McKernan, Jamie Creed, Connie Wagner,
Billy McDougall, Brittany Atwater,
and the rest of the Mount Desert Psychic Group

I have had a dream—past the wit of man to say what dream it was. Man is but an ass if he go about to expound this dream. Methought I was—there is no man can tell what. Methought I was, and methought I had—but man is but a patched fool if he will offer to say what methought I had. The eye of man hath not heard, the ear of man hath not seen, man's hand is not able to taste, his tongue to conceive, nor his heart to report what my dream was. I will get Peter Quince to write a ballad of this dream. It shall be called "Bottom's Dream" because it hath no bottom.

WILLIAM SHAKESPEARE,
A MIDSUMMER NIGHT'S DREAM,
ACT 4, SCENE 1, LINES 201–12

Contents

Foreword

By Sophie Strand

We rest our eyes on a photon and it blinks between process and punctuation, wave eternally gnawing at the shoreline and a raindrop prickle of singularity. But even worse, what happens when the photon looks at us? Do we turn particulate or oscillatory? As we observe, we increasingly realize we live in a world that is more verb than noun. We live in a "worlding" that observes and changes us in return. What happens when we create a double-slit experiment big enough that a plane of people can pass through? What happens when something as miniscule as a virus laces itself so tightly around the globe that we feel our cultural airways narrowing?

We live in uncertain times. We live in the dreaming of Heisenberg's Uncertainty principle itself, unsure whether as humans we are a climactic event or holobionts that pulse with perpetual becoming. The choppier the waters, the more we are drawn to answers that we can stand on like a desert island, isolating ourselves from the chaos that might ultimately be more generative.

Richard Grossinger cares little for answers. It is not often that someone of such poetic sensibility and erudition displays true humility and generosity of imagination. Modern science and politics are dominated by polemics. A position is articulated not by the depth and fertility of its thinking, but by its ability to demolish its opponents. Grossinger in

Dreamtimes and Thoughtforms offers us a radically different approach. F. Scott Fitzgerald wrote in his famous 1936 essay "Crack Up," "The test of a first-rate intelligence is the ability to hold two opposed ideas in the mind at the same time, and still retain the ability to function." But in a moment when the rate of cultural learning as aided by technology and connectivity far outpaces the ability of an individual to develop expertise, it might be amended that true intelligence it is the ability to hold a hundred opposing viewpoints in your mind.

An impossible task; and yet this is something that Grossinger accomplishes with little need for philosophical acrobatics. Rather he creates an ecosystem where fire salamanders and mermaids and quarks can all coexist and co-become. He presents the musings of zen masters and cab drivers with equal respect and interest. Most importantly, he centers the "ideas" of the world beyond human beings. Playfully, Grossinger summons a new pantheon for an age of ruptured ecologies and contaminated multiverses: tardigrades, crows, octopuses, microbiomes. We will not be saved by the sterile fiction of an individual who understands everything. But we might be well-nourished by the playful ability to inhabit different paradigms without passing judgment. Grossinger kaleidoscopes through the *umwelts* of non-human beings and through the psychospheric miasma of entangled ontologies.

Might I suggest that the real beauty of this book is that it presents an entirely new roadmap? A feral hermeneutics for an age of ecocide and cultural chaos. How can we use the DNA of acorns, the biomimicry of cephalopods, mating viruses, reports of extraterrestrial sightings, and psychic channels all to create an ecosystem of emergent ideas and "thoughtforms" rather than a gridlock of oppositions? Grossinger suggests, "Magical practice is not to make the world magical or *more* magical. The natural world is magical enough. Magic is to guide people through manifestations—it guides porcupines and sea urchins too." If magic is a guide then Grossinger's book represents a type of magic. It guides us gently into an interrogative mindset when the unfiltered onslaught of information threatens to drown us. It demonstrates how to generously inhabit different worlds, different beings, and different belief systems without subscribing to any of them.

"Try to love the questions themselves," the poet Ranier Maria Rilke advised. "The point is to live everything. Live the question now." In an age of climate change and coronavirus there are lessons to be learned and there are better dreams to be dreamed. But they do not necessarily belong to human beings. First, we must ask the right questions; and we must love the questions with such care and attention that they allow us to dream up other worlds. Our task is to develop an empathic muscularity toned by both tender curiosity and intellectual rigor. Flowing from cosmogenesis right into the advent of nanotechnology, this book is a lesson in living inside questions. It is the blurred moment when an electron leaps between energy levels. Unclassifiable. A map back to the fertile ground of your own magical uncertainty.

SOPHIE STRAND is a poet and writer with a focus on the history of religion and the intersection of spirituality, storytelling, and ecology. Her poems and essays have appeared in numerous projects and publications, including the Dark Mountain Project and poetry.org and the magazines *Unearthed, Braided Way, Art PAPERS,* and *Entropy.* She is the author of *The Flowering Wand: Rewilding the Sacred Masculine* and *The Madonna Secret.*

Acknowledgments

My thanks to editors Hazel Avery, Eliza Homick, and Jeanie Levitan and cover designer Aaron Davis for their indispensable contributions to this book. In addition, I want to thank the following people for dialogues that helped me shape the text: Matt McKay, Ron Sieh, Paul Weiss, Chuck Stein, Keith Thompson, Rachel Wolfe, Anthony Peake, Jeff Kripal, Miranda July, Richard Hoagland, Salicrow, Laura Aversano, Dewey Martin, Jonathan Cott, Charles Poncé, Patricia Cori, Luke Lafitte, Meryl Nass, Alexandra Whitney, Peter Levine, Ellias Lonsdale, Shea Rosenberg, and Barbara Karlsen.

PREFACE
Reading Gateway Cards

Cosmogenesis is the creation of universes. It is also Creation itself—Genesis—in every tradition and dimension, at every scale and echelon, as cosmoses and as what Tibetan lamas call "bardos," bridges between cosmoses or states of consciousness. Bardos were traditionally intermediate phases, in Himalayan lineages of Bonpo and Buddhism, between deaths and rebirths (reincarnations) during which consciousness occurs but is not attached to a physical body. As the concept was more deeply interrogated, the bardo after death proved no more definitive or transitional than many other bardos, including those of (1) waking life, (2) dreams, (3) entheogen-induced spells, (4) shamanic trance-journeys to other heavens, (4) astral, etheric, and higher-plane out-of-the body travel, (5) proprioception-altering illnesses, (6) epileptic, migranoid, and other seizures, (7) comas, (8) deep meditative reveries of insight, (9) near-death experiences, and (10) any transient state of euphoria, rapture, depression, terror, shock, or sustained hallucination. Bardos are themselves fully endowed—as bottomless, believable, and conditional in their framings as waking realms are to their habitants and vagabonds.

The subtler undertone is that consciousness moves between provisional states without discontinuity because "discontinuities" are equally states. Underlying this concept is an even deeper precept: that all worlds as well as all mind states arise from pristine awareness or pure consciousness transcending both thought and form, roughly defined by the Tibetan word *rigpa*. Reality, including the starry pavilion with all its worlds and phenomenologies, is a mirage, illusion, bubble, hallucination, reflection, duality—created by mind itself.

Creation arises from a primordial ground luminosity, a pure essence beyond concept or form. A hermit sits for days, months, or years in a cave in order to view this luminosity from a mortal body. A greater sun eventually rises within rather than across reality, illuminating it with the glow of existence, what it means for anything to be.

This meditation corresponds loosely to tarot trump nine of the Greater Arcana. The Hermit is a seeker guided by *rigpa,* the union of clarity and emptiness and the light of his or her own unconscious, which is borne in a lantern (or latency) and reflected in distant lone stars of a black, indigo, purple, or blue sky (depending on the tarot). The Hermit along with the Hierophant, Wheel, Tower, and Star are gateway cards. As other oracle decks are being drawn these days faster than spring clover, Fox, Clouds, a tetrahedron, a jovial breeze, archangel Michael, a dragon of deliverance, an iridium moon, an elephant spirit, and a sea priestess are among their gatekeepers.

I entitled a previous (1986) book of mine *Embryogenesis,* meaning how creatures enter this cosmos—nesting in cellulomolecular cocoons, then layering whirling-dervish-like in an egg, before incarnating as a sentient being. From an epistemological standpoint, embryogenesis *is* cosmogenesis, a roost in which spirit molts and re-forms, taking on carnal contour for Earth tenure. Universes manifest coordinately as mindedness, as quasi-material dynamic fields, and as views. Each is induced by each other into the truth mystery itself.

My premise is that reality is a manifestation, one of many. That doesn't demote the material universe to a *mere* illusion or hallucination with no solidity—for there are *only* insubstantial manifestations: a transdimensional tower of worlds and realms, stacked in tiers of frequencies or planes, through which karmically impelled souls transit. Mind is *senior* to matter. Mind is what *makes* matter into matter.

Realities are also not circumstantial. Even if manifestations, they are pearls on the same string, interrelated, earned, sequential. I side here with Native American spirit, Hindu *maya,* and the Australian

Aboriginal *alcheringa* or Dreamtime. By including the latter in my title, I am acknowledging an ancient, originary mode of clairsentient consciousness and tribal phenomenology. In the Dreamtime, the universe is magical, musical, and sung by all its entities together—we share a powerful, relevant, and active songline. Stuff going on anywhere affects stuff occurring everywhere and as anything.

Whatever arises in a physical universe is in shape-shifting verisimilitude with all other evolving universes across All That Is. This should cue you to the fact that the universe of science and its technocracy, while heralded as the cat's lone meow and singular hope of humanity, is a rinky-dink machine-shop cosmos driven by a card counter's algorithms. Moguls like J. Bezos, E. Musk, V. Putin, and B. Gates are temporarily beating the casino on its own terms, but the casino sits on a karmically arising grassland under an extension of uncertainty states, fractals, and strings of fine threads and rough cordage igniting one another transdimensionally. These guys won't win indefinitely.

Baseline phenomena (stars, stones, seas, and weather) are transpositions of conditions elsewhere. Like states of the human psyche (self, anima, hero, trickster), they originate in what psychologist Carl Jung called archetypes. Archetypes are motifs that span bardos. We cannot say what their primal forms are, for we know them only by aspects they display on any one planet in any one epoch in any one observable cosmos.

On latter-day Earth, physics, chemistry, astronomy, psychology, anthropology, mathematics, and thermodynamics are spatiotemporal sciences, but they are also subsets of archetypal or traditionary sciences like alchemy, astrology, shamanism, numerology, and magic. Each traditionary science represents an organizing principle that exists in Creation at large, outside the Big Bang, in every latent and manifest universe.

The ultimate universal laws are unknowable in any one nervous system or by any single type of ganglion and mind. In this regard, a human philosopher is no savvier than a grasshopper or wren.

From their local expressions, we can interpolate the domains of archetypal sciences. Alchemy explores transitions between phases of manifestation. In a thermodynamic alembic, these regulate transmutations of mind and matter. Terrestrial alchemists work toward conjunctions of elemental substances, seeking crossover states and their phenomenologies. Alchemy also encompasses tiers of causal energy that give rise regionally to tables, periodicities, octaves, and isotopes.

The line between psyche and substance fluctuates, for *both* were a thoughtform in the solar cloud. There, mind and matter were inseparable and indistinguishable. All consciousness was telekinetic; all mass-and-motion mind-driven. Thoughtforms continue to arise in cooler, slower space-time: a lamp, a cabin, or a train's caboose is a thoughtform, a thought turned into a form as well as a shift-potential shape.

Modern chemists and physicists, by contrast, confine their tracking to molecular properties emergent on Earth and, from spectrographic analyses, on exotic planets and stars.

Astrology is the concomitant cosmography and psychology of All That Is. In the "birth" chart of every animate and inanimate being as well as each occasion, destinies are individualized—individuated—against all contingencies and states of singularity. Because each multiverse forms against the backdrop of *all* multiverses—All That Is—their meanings are organized by coincidings and synchronicities. That's why zodiacal charts "work" even multi-centrically. There are no wrong divinations or contexts, only different ways of telling the same story or fortune.

The stars that we see index another star-field within yet another, and another, each with multiple centricities and frames of reference. This enfolded para-celestial background holds universes in place. Because each universe forms against the backdrop of all universes, their sigils are bound to superior (interior) fields. Each zodiac dowses that hyperspatial whirlpool while each astronomy sets its near levers, gears, cycles, and screens. That is why there is finally an orbiting planet, centaur, or asteroid to dot every "i" and cross every "t."[1]

One could argue that thermodynamics and astrology are yoked to each other by gravity and synchronicity, which are expressions of one energy at different frequencies. Psychologist Carl Jung and physicist Wolfgang Pauli tried to cut that Gordian knot together with marginal success; see *Atom and Archetype: The Pauli-Jung Letters, 1932–1958*.

The driver behind all this is karma, though not "karma" as we bandy the word in pop parlance. Karma is gravity and mass working in concert with psyche and being. It is how everything, conscious and unconscious, enacts cosmoses together. Bardos hatch because they have to. Our physical domain, what we call "nature" (from the Greek *gnascari*—"to be born" plus the future participle *urus*) is not only a transfigured *gnosis* but a continuous nativity. All worlds work together to complete—*complete* is not the word—a grand experiment of interim clarities. Creation models the athanors of Renaissance alchemists more than the centrifuges of successor chemists, for the periodic table is confined to one range of collisions and their outcomes, whereas All That Is is exploring mixed media.

There are finally no *real* things, only thoughtforms: modules flowing through minded states into manifestations. Soul driven, evolving, generating entire universes, they answer the eternal question "Which came first?"—by "Neither." There is no distinction between mind and matter, thought and form, goose and egg. The physics and biology of the universe—the laws of *gnature*—are a thoughtform seeking its own basis and discovering *what* it is by expressing it.

Dreamtimes and Thoughtforms begins by addressing our landed universe and its dioceses, particularly the origin and destiny of sentient beings on Planet Earth as well as, presumably, elsewhere in the cosmos. My life-long inquiry into this topic began with riffs in my early twenties in the mid-1960s that led to *Solar Journal: Oecological Sections,* and proceeded through works like *Spaces Wild and Tame; Book of the Earth and Sky; The Long Body of the Dream;* and *The Slag of Creation.* In 1975, I changed genres from experimental prose to expository narrative; e.g., from pure dowsing to topic-driven matrices like this one.

Dreamtimes and Thoughtforms directly follows my book *Bottoming Out the Universe: Why There Is Something Rather Than Nothing,* which itself advances themes from a three-volume work I called *Dark Pool of Light: Reality and Consciousness,* the first on the neuroscience and ontology of consciousness, the second on consciousness in psychic and psychospiritual ranges, the third on the crisis and future of consciousness. Those four books—2010 to 2020—rest on my previous (1977 to 2003) series: *Planet Medicine* (*Origins* and *Modalities* volumes); *The Night Sky: Soul and Cosmos*; *Embryogenesis: Species, Gender, and Identity*; and *Embryos, Galaxies, and Sentient Beings: How the Universe Makes Life*. From 2003 to 2010, I wrote a companion trilogy: *On the Integration of Nature* (2005), *The Bardo of Waking Life* (2008), and *2013: Raising the Earth to the Next Vibration* (2010).

I am a literary writer—sorry, "science only" readers. My explorations in physics, biology, paraphysics, and mysticism came after my teen meetings with John Keats, Herman Melville, and William Faulkner.

I am also an occult writer. I read tarot cards at sixteen and presently help shepherd a psychic group on Zoom (per my dedication) These meet (the literary and occult). For me the occult is occulted (and revealed) by phonetics as well as semantics. That is, content isn't its own only source of meaning. Form is an extension of content.

After reading a late draft of *Dreamtimes and Thoughtforms,* one rad scientist interested in "microtubular signal transduction" and "deciphering the code of the morphogenetic field" (as I am) wrote back that my writing was "as always, verbose and unduly self-enamored and self-impressed." That startled and stung. I *am* enamored of voices and, if I am impressed, it is by them, their strangeness and variety, not by any choreography of my own.

Some minds work best by assault and dialectic, so I appreciate his ding. It was helpful like a Zen slap or windshield ticket. Whether it is accurate isn't up to me. I write as I write, and the alternative is not *to write as someone else writes* (or asks me to write) but not to write at all. I am glad that the microtubular guy also warned me about what he called my "endless alliteration of everything." I agree. Where it occurs, it is stupefying, almost bizarre.

I am not a traditional alliterator or lister; in fact, I have scrupulously avoided Longfellow-like lyricisms and meters. I consider alliteration a cheap trick, a crossword-puzzle-like game best for pop librettos where it is carried by melody. Yet the more I wrote this book, the more it alliterated and the more it also felt channeled. By that, I don't mean that I heard an alien voice or spoke in tongues, but I also don't *not* mean those. I began to hear sounds of sentences ahead of or along with their meanings and, after a while, I began to listen and record. I agree that it can sound like self-enamorment, but I believe it is something else: an older, not entirely contemporary English voice speaking along with me, a bit Elizabethan, a bit mock-academic, not undue but ornate and dense as if a Sirian narrator were talking Gaian. Sorry, rad scientist. I heard it that way.

Here's what I think: when one flips into an interdimensional message, its language reflects its source of transmission. Words that list toward etymology and onomatopoeia expedite a "transduction" (microtubular yes, necessarily) of sound into meaning. I decided to encourage instead of fighting it once I realized that long tallies and alliterations are signatures of a meta-language or information set (like multi-spirt Seth's Sumari). Singsong though it is, glossolalia accompanies us out of the Great Void.

I initially composed *Dreamtimes and Thoughtforms* within a larger text. I have tentatively named its more secular part *The Return of the Tower of Babel: QAnon, COVID, and Chaos Magic*. Together, the titles make a twin tablet of cosmological and political auguries that began in a source folio, *Reading Gateway Cards: Opening the 2020 Portal*.

"Gateway Cards" intimates that Earth is passing through a portal in space-time. Overdue oracles are hatching: 1987's harmonic convergence, the Common Era's Y2K, 2012's end to the Mayan calendar and our solar system's convergence with the galactic center, and the zodiacal Age of Aquarius scintillate together now like the tail of a rattlesnake. It has become hard to tell a nation from a barony, a world power from a failed state.

Even with meticulously managed clocks and data clouds, time no longer sticks to gears, ticks, or cesium atoms; it has become distended, longer and thicker, even stalling out, in some precincts, while whipping by like a solar wind in others. Distance has warped too, from the farthest nebulae to getting crosstown. Urban zones and their malls and eateries have distended like Salvador Dali clocks, while individuals—in Hong Kong, Cape Town, Buenos Aires, and Boise—sat together in Zoom cafés.

Meanwhile, a hollow has been growing at the core of civilization, beyond context or meaning. While the modern world is churning out trillion-fold algorithms, bitcoins, and bling, it is untethered to a tribe or soul.

Astrologers and clairvoyants sensed something huge out there but didn't know what it was. Like a planet-killing comet or system-perturbing "Planet X," it kept getting vaster and emptier, camouflaged by the digital dazzle of the Kuiper belt. Texture and life were being drained from the world and replaced by an artificially sweetened, deficit-funded substitute. The Inuit spoke of a shift in the Earth's orbit: "The sun is in a different place now," their elders said. "Everything is tilting northward. The winds are fitful, weather unpredictable." They checked with other elders; they agreed, something big is happening.

In 2017, a cigar-shaped object of anomalous trajectory whipped through our System, changing speed and albedo in ways that Newtonian comets can't. It was gone before astronomers realized they had a black swan, an unpiloted foo. They failed to resolve its signature and decode its nature. Too late! The elongated rod was on its way toward Pegasus.

The misidentified comet, dubbed 'Oumuamua after Hawaiian for "scout" because it was first observed at twenty-one million miles (or 0.22 AU: Gaia-Sun units) from the Haleakalā Observatory in Maui, broke the plane of the Solar System on September 6 from the direction of Vega twenty-five light years away, reached perihelion on September 9, and was out of range a month later.

When Harvard astronomer Avi Loeb proposed that the interstellar object might not have been another surplus rock but the first techno-signature from away—debris from one of the many civilizations in the universe, perhaps a light-driven sail several kilometers long and only a few millimeters thick, perhaps a camera probe—he was all but excommunicated from the guild.[2]

Where was NASA's asteroid watch? It was busy charting Apophis in 2029.

Evolutionary astrologer and ayahuasquero Laura Matsue declared, "2020 is like the world is in an ayahuasca ceremony together—and most people have neither prepared for it nor do they even know they're in it and there's no shaman. The shaman is meant to create some containment around the energy of the ceremony, and there's definitely none of that going on."[3]

Instead, we have the shaman of no-shaman.

ONE

Planet

BIG BANG

The Big Bang came first, that's the canonical audit of science. It preceded the star-spangled universe, perhaps the multiverse too. By "multiverse" I mean a panoply of probable and parallel universes issuing from the same particle point. Maybe there were many particle points, "big bangs," and creationary events.

Either way, what preceded a big bang? What cast gravity, heat, and mass across curvature into scalar magnitude? What caused "cause"?

To appearances, the Big Bang was an explosion (or implosion) that transcended terms for either because it spread only into space and time it created—it did not occur *in* them (or in anything); it *made* them. After imploding, it continued to pop like corn—hydrogen nebulae—in its own "oil," liquefied radiations. It subsumed any conventional blast, yielding runes we call preons, quarks, strings, and particles, forging atoms and then molecules, as it fused and fissioned across the void. Except how can there be an alcove called "void" without an amphitheater called "space"?

Everything in objective creation came from the initial fissioning: meteors, hair dryers, frogs. Adjudicating chaos and containment, it created ground and sky and set countless cyclotrons and pendula aligning across worlds.

The flames haven't died down yet. Fourteen billion Earth-Sol orbits later, embers are still spasming and spit firing. It was a clown car from which the clowns never stopped coming. In the process, it exponentialized, metastasized, and incubated, spawning compound yarn: hadrons, fermions, and cinders that kept fissuring and combining as they hopped tiers, yielding paramecia, mosquito eggs, dandelion seeds, plankton, supernovas.

This rummage of undetermined scale organized at intervals of an Arabic and Roman ten (decimal), an Egyptian twelve (duodecimal), a Sumerian sixty (sexagesimal), and far greater ordinals and powers. Cosmologist Nassim Haramein notes coefficients joining helix-shaped nebulae to the helical eyeballs that view them, between mitoses of cells and deaths of stars, between a synaptic map of brain cells and a synoptic glyph of the *entire* observable cosmos. Underground mycelial webs—fibers of fungal life—foreshadow fiber-optic networks, an infinity of roads and their cul-de-sacs.

Likewise, a sunflower on Sol 3 mimes its namesake star. Its young inflorescence, or composite flower, follows solar rays, as its seed-swarm grows in an occult Fibonacci spiral. The brown-red disk of mature florets and bright yellow sepals then cast a replica of the sun during total lunar eclipse.[1]

As above, so below. Eridanus, a river of stars, flows into the intestines of a salmon.

As galaxies spew out stars, stars breed particles, elements knit compounds, compounds become organisms. The universe is a chain of self-similar superpositions—a scalar undulation, budding and spurting where ripe, posting its blueprint onto time. As galactic spirals sow double-helix codes, gonads swell with gametes, gametes activate embryogenic fields, plants and animals clone fresh cells and semen, galaxies ignite new suns and spores. Every bird and snake re-lays the Cosmic Egg.

When Freudian orgonomist Wilhelm Reich sourced passion in primordial hydrogen, he presaged *all* plants and animals too. Howling cats in heat proffer the same superimposition as rings of Saturn or a crab nebula. He meant that nature is a libidinal splurge—it had to be in order to express both ground luminosity and dialectical depth. Buildup of creature excitation in orgasm perpetuates the creationary spark, as it continues to expand from an encapsulated particle to a far-flung recursion. Hydrogen—hermetic mercury—fissions into electrons and protons while dimensionalizing into suns and seeds. All That Is had an innate "desire" to dilate, differentiate, and complexify—to release its pent-up charge. It dissolves matter in its own liqueur as it assuages *its erotic curiosity about itself.*

The Big Bang foreshadowed the Freudian-Jungian unconscious—an archetypal estuary gushing into rendition as reaction formation* and revelation: yin and yang.

Several riddles are posed by a "big bang":

- If a single particle smaller than a jujube chundered all of creation, from where did it get its material, let alone mechanism and laws? If gravity and curvature preceded *it,* WTF are gravity and curvature?
- Was our big bang a pregnant photon that splintered instantly into a holographic universe? Does that explain the façade of galaxies to its wee partisans within?
- If time, space, and space-time *had to be inaugurated,* what preconditioned them? And how can anything be before "before" or *malgré* time?
- And who killed cock robin? Did mindedness *pre*exist? Did karma qua gravity require an implosion, whipping up worlds to deliver failed imperatives of prior worlds, or was it pure dada? Did it implode physically or liminally or both? Who will toll the bell and carry the coffin?

Is the universe, in the sense of All That Is, a thoughtform or a chemistry set? Is it a spree of adventitious algorithms that, given space enough and time, can create anything from yesterday's residue—a play of particles aggregating *ex post facto,* fashioning Legos into earwigs, rubies,

---

*Reaction formation (from Sigmund Freud's *Reaktionsbildung*) is a defense mechanism similar to Carl Jung's enantiodromia: emotional anxiety is reduced by exaggerating its opposite tendency—things turn naturally into their antipodes.

and comets? Or is it a thoughtform ricocheting in its own reflection? I will address the notion that it is both, *simultaneously and reciprocally*, throughout this book.

A different mode of origin is adduced by the Hebrew Zohar's Tree of Life: As transdimensional rays cascaded from Kether, the cosmogonic gateway and crown, their "hidden" light responded to a primal stirring of Ein Soph, the unmanifested Divine, giving a laical big bang a bottomless dowry. The implosion was seminally alphabetic and algebraic, stem to stern, pillar to post. It translated words and numbers from one dimension to another.

Astrophysicist Brian Swimme rechristened the Big Bang the "Primordial Flaring Forth," to take weaponry and mischief out of it and restore a covenant of Greek and Egyptian theogonies.[2] Swimme's metaphor isn't just semantic, it shifts motive: a sacred emanation as opposed to an improvised pipe device, Paul Simon's *"days of miracle and wonder"* and *"long distance call"* instead of his *"bomb in the baby carriage wired to the radio."*[3]

A Primordial Flaring Forth jives, verse by verse, with Genesis, whereas a Big Bang is God's Second Amendment firing range.

As particles scattered in the frontal flare, they stirred a cauldron they had melded, thinning into its frontiers, clustering around gravitational centers—galaxies—because remember, gravity was already there.

Gravity, the Greek god Apocalypse—literally "a disclosure of information"—is the lone surviving deity from a prior pantheon, the missing son of Kronos (Time) and Rhea (Great Mother), twin brother to Zeus (Harvest), grandson of Gaia (Ground) and Ouranos (Space). That's pre-Socratic physics from the Stone Ages.

Apocalypse is a cardinal deity, able to disrobe into thermodynamics without revealing a pothole or pore. His shadows—heat, shear, mass, momentum—spread into nooks and crannies like plum jam. In kimonos of dark energy and matter, he is able to touch everything in his domain and make everything touch everything else. Stuffing itself into each mote and crevice, bending space-time without divulging a farthing, gravity divests not just knowledge but a lesion in knowing reenacted by philosophers like Jacques Derrida, Jacques Lacan, and Gilles Deleuze.

The Primal Flare exceeded an unthinkable 1,000 trillion degrees Celsius. As gamma-ray embers plunged from its athanor into the *nigredo* of interstellar night, the Flare's unconscious contents began to take shape, creating Nut—Sky—a backdrop of multiple firmaments and heavens.

After many *kalpas,* a newbie disc—a proto-sun—purled from the Milky Way Nebula, spinning as it swept curds out of Rhea's cream, molten hydrogen at still more than 6,000 degrees Kelvin. Its children would call it Ra, Helios, Surya, Sol, Huītzilōpōchtli, Wuriupranili.

At the core of the spinning spiral were the two most abundant elements in the galaxy, hydrogen and helium. As their molten sog coalesced, outer chunks of the greater cloud, drawn to each other by gravity, accreted into planetesimals, whirling stones of a thousand-or-so meters diameter—archaeoastronomy's protoplanets.

Around 700 BCE, Greek poet Hesiod dead-reckoned the system's birth throes from fifty thousand years of unwritten Pleistocene cosmogeny:

> First Kaos (Chaos) came to be, but next wide-bosomed Gaia (Earth), the ever-sure foundations of all the deathless ones who hold the peaks of snowy Olympus and dim Tartaros in the depth of the wide-pathed Gaia, and Eros (Love), fairest among the deathless gods, who unnerves the limbs and overcomes the mind and wise counsels of all gods and all men within them. From Kaos came forth Erebos, [the shadow, and dark Nyx (Night)]; but of Nyx were born Aether (Bright Sky) and Hemera (Day), whom she conceived and bore from union in love with Erebos. And Gaia first bore starry Ouranos (Heaven), equal to herself, to cover her on every side.[4]

It was as romantic as it was torrid, for its time a Bollywood sitcom.

In Navajo Nation's cosmogenesis, Asdzą́ą́ Nádleehé (Changing Woman) grew from the union of Long Life Boy and Happiness Girl.

Literally the "woman who changes," she used pieces of her own exfoliated skin and a medicine bundle made of mountain soil and buckskin to fashion four couples, ancestors of the four Navajo clans.

Sol warmed its eggery like a giant tern. Nearer ova simmered at 2,000 Kelvin, while the outer nest cooled to a tepid 50 units. Inner worlds did not draw as many curds as median orbs, so they bundled in smaller spheres and formed hard surfaces. On primeval Mercury, Venus, Earth, Mars, Ceres, Vesta, Pallas, and other planetoids, micro-fields with high melting points consolidated. Their molecules precipitated into minerals and metals, crusts and scarps—our sort of real estate.

Meanwhile, lighter protons vaporized as they formed hyperspheres under gravity. Digital close-ups of Jupiter and Saturn today look both cellular and like magnificent marbles, a moving portfolio of every canvas that Jackson Pollack and Hilma af Klimt could ever paint given eternal time and dyes.

Beyond the asteroid belt—the system's frost line—even lighter molecules solidified. Electromagnetic cores of what would become Uranus and Neptune as well as Jupiter and Saturn continued to attract hydrogen and helium, as they amasssed initially into rapidly rotating gasballs, great fleece of rainbow cotton candy surrounded by rings and moons. Larger Jovian satellites were named Titan, Europa, Enceladus, Callisto, Miranda, Ganymede, Janus, Ariel, Umbriel, Triton, Ophelia by the European world that discovered them. Their Olympian-Shakespearian kingdom seized the preponderance of angular momentum projected by Sol and their own gathering bodies. Springs of a local zodiac got wound.

In Sol's inner system, iron, silicon, magnesium, sulfur, aluminum, calcium, nickel, and their elemental neighbors crystallized. While oxygen remained gaseous, some of its molecules bonded into rocks as they cooled. One "stone" was unique. Oxidizing the universe's lightest and most abundant particle—hydrogen with an atomic weight at par (1.008)—water molecules fluctuated in round square-dances, hydrogens continuously displacing one another and bonding with new oxygens. As the ionized atoms oscillated, they trapped their own energy while absorbing external heat. Instead of boiling off, as their kind did nearer Sol on Venus and Mercury, oxidized hydrogens made aqueous flow on Gaia and Mars. Its squirts were viscous, resilient, electrically conductive—ubiquitous.[5]

As splash pelted stone, a planet-size sauna sent steam upward into an icy flask, the union of Ouranos and Aether. It deliquesced back with lightning and thunder. Large and small cracks filled with H_2O, making streams, bays, basins, oceans, lakes, torrential rivers.

During this phase of geogenesis, a Mars-size asteroid crashed into Gaia, ejecting a chunk of her mantle into near space where it congealed as a separate subordinal body, Luna. Obedient to terrestrial gravity while imposing a lunar yoke, the satellite brought Earth's carousing winds and waters to heel, taming runaway cyclones into weather and tides, setting the stage for a biosphere and noosphere. It died as a world while converting into a metronome and valve. A photo of Luna orbiting Earth from NASA's Deep Space Climate Observatory shows an ashen gray floating boulder casting a spell on a waterworld and garden fifty times its size.

The seminal rogue asteroid was later named Theia after the Greek mother of Selene, goddess of the moon—a play of imaginal astrophysics and retro-mythology. She is thought to have wandered from the outer Solar System or to have long accompanied proto-Earth in near orbit before being perturbed by neighboring Venus or giant Jupiter. After the collision, Theia became part of Gaia, contributing her minerals to its core, her waters to its surface and atmosphere. We are Theians as well as Terrans.

While this hullabaloo was taking place in matter, its counterpart was propagating causal energy in spirit spheres. Landscapes forming out of molten molecules complemented liminal continents like Atlantis and Lemuria.

The birth of sun and moon and life forms, proposed turn-of-the-twentieth-century occult philosopher Rudolf Steiner, emulated parallel evolutions in planes outside of time and space. While matter reached up (or out) to spirit—in a quartz crystal as well as an emergent crab—spirit reached down (or in) to cast a material substrate from its essence.

While physical Earth matriculated by geological epochs—Cambrian, Ordovician, Silurian, Devonian, Eocene—esoteric Earth underwent correlative metamorphoses: Polarean, Hyperborean, Lemurian, and Atlantean phases marked our progenitors' pilgrimages from Astral to Etheric to Physical bodies. These states comprise bardos through which souls were gradually deeded bodies. They passed from vapors to fire mists to water to flesh—metaphorically from Saturn to Sun to Moon to Earth—and from mineral deposits to the plant kingdom to invertebrate and reptile mazes to mammalian jurisdictions.

Anthroposophy is Steiner's name for his meta-science of soul history. He derived it by meditations on the Akashic Chronicle, his interpretation of psychically inscribed tablets that record every event throughout all universes. These nonphysical annals of All That Is are only accessible telepathically.[6]

Luna's separation from Earth was Astral, then Etheric, then physical and astronomical. An astral/astrological drama in the macrocosm mirrored the space collision in the microcosm. In Steiner's cosmology, every zygote and larva reenacts Terran-Lunar transformation; every caterpillar or eel emanates through phases of separation and renewal. Ontogeny, phylogeny, and cosmogony—egg, embryo, and cosmos—likewise recapitulate one another again and again because nothing else compasses them. Steiner explains:

> The soul or astral ancestors of man were transported to the refined or etheric earth. . . . [T]hey sucked the refined substance into themselves like a sponge, to speak coarsely. By thus becoming penetrated with substance, they developed etheric bodies. These had an elongated elliptical form, in which the limbs and other organs which were to be formed later were already indicated by delicate shadings of the substance. All processes in this mass were purely physical-chemical, but they were regulated and dominated by the soul. . . .
>
> Up to this point there had been no material separation between sun, earth, and moon. In their effect on man these three were one body. Now the separation took place; the more delicate substantiality, which includes everything which had previously made it possible

for the soul to act in an immediately vitalizing manner, separated itself as the sun; the coarsest part was extruded as the moon; and the earth, with respect to its substantiality, stood in the middle between the two others.[7]

The soul—cosmic, group, and personal—needed space to grow.

ICE

Steam continued to descend from Nut as rain, snow, and sleet; it rolled as mists through valleys and as fog off bays. Its crystals accumulated in hail and icebergs. Glaciers roared from polar caps down rivulets, moving rocks and alps, feeding rivers and seas. Water froze on the surfaces of lakes and kettle ponds, insulating them for more nuanced chemistry.

Then water did something amazing: it came alive. The Vedas say that it drew spirit from the Etheric aspect of the solar cloud. In modern occult terms, it percolated from Steiner's astral and etheric realms or from Teilhard's nascent noosphere,* bonding with carbon and nitrogen to form acids of a contiguous, contagious code. RNA molecules portend the first tablets of their own literature, to be written on cave walls, papyruses, and electron screens, to be cawed by crows, spun by bees and spiders, flashed by octopuses. These are forerunners of linguist Noam Chomsky's generative grammars. Parakeet, Bonobo, Inupiaq, Quechua, Ibo, Icelandic, Japanese, and HTML are neuroaffectively a single tongue.

Water, as well as compounds of carbon and hydrogen—methanes, ethanes—forge humongous "ice" castles, cathedrals, and megapolises. Beyond stars' frost lines, these comprise whole continents of worlds like Callisto, Enceladus, and Titan. Hydrocarbons are so abundant throughout the universe that they aggregate into crystal-ball planets around other stars. Their occult histories proceed along different trajectories from ours.

As its atoms shapeshifted in states of electron probability, water

---

*For the noosphere, see the works of French archaeologist-priest Pierre Teilhard de Chardin, particularly his *Phenomenon of Man*.

was destined to become aqua—or an elemental—at Gaia's octave. In its solid phase, it is the most prolific crystal in the geosphere: glacier, icicle, snowflake, hail, sleet, lake-skin, lapidem, microtubule. In its liquid form, it rushes, steeps, and sublimates as elixirs, springs, lagoons, rivulets, raindrops. Its vapors yield cerations and sublimations: troposphere, cloud, fog, humidity, and a sylph's kiss of dew. In its native Astral plane, it personifies into undines and merfolk.

Water's Physical-Etheric field sponsors fractal incarnations: amoeba to whale, rotifer to cat, ctenophore to manatee.

Aqua also mediates heat and absence of heat: star ovens and the interstellar void. Cold is technically "quantum-mechanical zero-point energy-induced particle motion" (or motionlessness)—the status of parsecs of dayless night where things go slower than a tortoise with an L. L. Bean pack and are chillier than the figurative well-digger's ass. At its deepest collection centers, gravity's star furnaces warmed spoors of unfigured rock and kicked up thousands-of-miles-per-hour winds. Sol's third planetesimal provided a rare moody blend, an "exquisitely protective crucible" commingling cold and hot, harmony and clatter, as oracular novelist Whitley Strieber eulogizes:

> So a benign star in a benign galaxy, a planet the perfect distance from its star and a moon in orbital balance with it are what enabled life to arise and evolve here. . . . [Yet] 99% of all species that have ever existed are now extinct, and there have been five great mass extinctions. The third one, the Permian mass extinction which happened 248 million years ago, killed 96% of all species then alive. Everything living now, including us, is descended from the 4% that survived. . . .
>
> [W]e are in the midst of a 6th mass extinction. The stage for it was set when the current ice epoch began . . . the Quaternary Glaciation, which started 2.8 million years ago. During that period, the ice has expanded and retreated many times, with each ice age lasting about 100,000 years. They are punctuated by interglacials, and we are at the end of one of these right now. . . .

Interglacials generally climax with a dramatic temperature spike . . . followed by equally sudden cooling. The heating is caused by the release of tremendous amounts of methane "frozen" in hydrates beneath the northern oceans. When the hydrates melt, which occurs at 47 degrees Fahrenheit, trillions of tons of methane gas escape into the atmosphere.[8]

Each shift of Gaia's climate triggered an extinction event leading to a parade of new species marching through Ordovician and Triassic time: trilobites, clams, pinworms, insects, turtles, cavies, dinosaurs, pterodactyls, boars, mastodons, turkey vultures; shrews, canines, felines, hyraxes, narwhals, echidnas, antelopes, goats, bats, jays, spiders, toads, mantises, ticks, capybaras. Fluctuations during briefer Pliocene and Pleistocene swings hatched bipeds: hominoid and hominid forebears. Adapting to swings of temperature, Australopithecine and Pithecanthropine packs turned into Neanderthal bands and Cro-Magnon tribes. Each glacial deviation initiated new lineages: hunters, shamans, bards, chiefs, kings, queens, witches, fisherfolk, captains, logicians, troglodytes, tricky holy women, masters of the potlatch and kula ring.

Ice floes, floods, and firestorms spun the vast sublime behind the origin myths of Gaia. "Across the universe," Strieber infers, "this has happened many times and consciousness looks at itself now in billions of different ways, through the eyes of countless minds. . . . The stress brought on by the continuous changes in climate of the current period are intended to speed up evolution on Earth."[9]

We should not forget that our current climate crisis will continue to draw on the biosphere's evolutionary potential.

Of course, we do not know what has been happening here or elsewhere. We see reality through a set of ectodermally-derived peepholes. Either we are on a humongous, inflated curve teeming with strange attractors—or we are in a dreamlike spheroidal mirage. The first astronauts looked homeward at a blue, cloud-mottled crystal spinning in space and time, posing as if a 3-D postcard. No other planet on this plane looks like Sol 3: a creature in its own taxonomy, ascending somewhere between 5- and 12-D. Don't be fooled by the solar census—this is a gerrymandered cryptid.

CLIMATE

In the Primal Flare, Ice and Fire were reciprocal, for fission (thermochemistry) requires abysm (flask). Hot and cold are later phenomenologies—stars know only faster and slower.

On Earth, Vulcan's forge was regulated by an older Greek goddess Chione spreading frosts of her girdle. In the Holocene, Chione's ice-pack, a thermostatic frock with semiconducting naiads maintained a stable temperature regime. Diodes of water and air recalled, withheld, and released packs of moderating molecules from permafrost.

Our planet's atmosphere trapped just the right quota of sunlight for photosynthesis, turning photons into energy through green arts of Chloris. The nymph of botany provided chlorophyll from her magnesium palette. Algae and her daughters sheltered land and sea—all of Gaia—outgassing flasks of delicious air.

Permafrost continues to regulate a civilization-friendly climate. The last major glaciers retreated from Earth's equator to its poles to end Pleistocene winter in an equally epochal Holocene spring. After Mesolithic floods, ancestors of boat- and stilt-hut peoples built metropolises at Ur and Tenōchtitlan. Thousands of orbits later, we celebrate their festive busk.

Crafts and symbols led to codices, dialectics, and civilizations, which installed devotions of sun, moon, and stars. Winds and waters delivered were-beasts and gods whose masks were as mutable as Otter and Raven, Isis and Horus, Titans and a pre-Zeusian dynasty. Whether these arose from our own astrum or an archetypal commons, they joined Gaia's human tribes and haunted their trails and settlements. Deities anchored clans and sodalities to prairies, savannas, rainforests, taigas, outbacks, archipelagos, deserts, tundras, urbs. Chiefdoms, papacies, and lodges amalgamated into the corporate hegemons of our postmodern Olympus.

Gaia and Sol still rule this emanation. Though demoted to great bags of deaf and dumb atoms, they still issue templates and temples, tabernacles and tenements from which a service rises to greet its priests. Dzogchen master Khenchen Palden Sherab conjures holy ground:

> It is as vast as the sky and as deep as the ocean. Great masters flew in the sky by exploring the depth of its meaning. In fact, every Nyingmapa and all other Buddhist practitioners are currently flying in the sky, whether they recognize it or not. Yet everyone flies according to their capabilities. Birds such as vultures fly high in the sky. Smaller birds, like crows, also fly in the sky. And even butterflies and moths fly in the sky! The fly flies, the moth flies, the bird flies, and vultures and eagles all fly. Accordingly, each and every being is exploring the sky. Though its depths are infinite, the nature of the sky is the same no matter where you touch it; there is no real difference to explore, because the sky just keeps going in all directions! That is how the nature is. All of us are flying according to our best capabilities as we explore the meaning of the Secret Essence Tantra.[10]

And so it is—we fly in vessels and cabs according to our cloaks and capabilities. Octopuses, crows, and ospreys span the Astral overlay and Essence Tantra in their own costumes, flying and swimming with us.

Hominids fashioned levees, spillways, railways, dams, factories, cities, suburbs, and exurbs, as they connected them by rails and electrical lines. They birthed a capital-generating infrastructure: factories, towns, burghs. Labor unions won middle-class lives for their rank and file. Prosperity spread, if inequitably, across Gaia.

After a second global clash, a liberalizing elite, presuming itself permanent and progressive, raised its sprat to believe in happy endings, as they conferred institutions and ideals on a postmodern arcade. With the fall of the Iron Curtain, the end of history was declared by neo-cons and neo-libs alike: a tech utopia of computer simulations, commodity lots, and virtual realities—a transhumanist cornucopia. Capitalist and socialist nations colluded on infinite freedom: bubble worlds controlled by politicos, marketing groups, and their myrmidons. One day, its archons proposed, Africa, Asia, and planets throughout the universe would join the Confederation.

Progressive liberalism never questioned its universal applicability, by United Nations or *Starship Enterprise*.

Rachel Carson warned us—and high schoolers read *Silent Spring*—but bozos didn't get that it applied to them, that it superseded party time, Coors, and horseplay.

We have entered what ecologists term "an Anthropocene back loop." Melting glaciers and superstorms churn into molecular grinding of waters and winds, as they receive plastic, metal, gas, and laboratory spill-off, hangover of a Renaissance blowout. Mass-produced amphoras of oil-based plastics, meters of fishing nets, cylinders, molds, and blisters of rubbery petroleums, trihalomethane refrigerants, lubricants, styro-foams, cellophanes, solvents, plugs, clips, clamps, and PFOAs conjugate with bacteria, worms, viruses, cosmetics, suntan lotions, pharmaceuti-cals, raw sewage, strip metals, and industrial ash. As xenophyophores, krill, and sea grasses feed on microplastics, rusts, and rots—pesticides and opiates enter food chains.[11]

Mass extractions continue to scoop and thaw Chione's crystal, singeing her arboreal mane, turning pastures and forests into erosional strips, exhuming methane hydrates and viruses, summoning the polar vortex into the bull ring. Eight billion of our species, armed with weap-ons of mass and regional destruction, imprison and butcher other life forms for their chow and board, begetting morgues and cesspools, exud-ing hydrocarbons, filling Astral spheres with suffering.

Undines and sylphs are abandoning sharks, white buffalo, kanga-roos, bees, and other Dreamtime suits. The aboriginal hunter lay down beside the great bird he had killed, put his head on its body, and said, "Thank you Brother Emu, Sister Emu, for sharing yourself and feeding us. Your spirit will always be with us and part of our tribe."[12]

He has been replaced by pigs in feeding troughs, chickens on guil-lotines, salmon birthed and raised in their waste. Village-size ships equipped with artificial intelligence are dispatched by merchants from China, Thailand, Timor, Japan, Indonesia. These floating factories drag the ocean floor, converting protoplasm into capital, discarding twenty times in bycatch their tuna, herring, shellfish, and cod. Coast dwellers in Africa are driven into jungles for sustenance—the fish and shellfish are gone. They consume monkeys, pangolins, civets, lizards, bats; they spread Ebola, cryptosporidia, paramyxoviruses, HIV. Is it any wonder that our algorithm found us, at Mosul, Abu Ghraib, and Wuhan?

Ice is still caucusing, healing, nectaring, transmuting. Weather systems tied to climate and driven by chaos variables are subject to thought-forms of watery creatures throughout Gaia's niches and habitats. Not enough credit is given to how minds unbalance nature. At 60 percent water, we attune to its octave as flower essence, tincture, sweat lodge, baptism, anointment, pulse, disturbance, quake. The traditional rain dance may be stifled by greenhouse gases, but it breathes in re-oaking, sylvan heat breaks, solar panels, wildlife corridors, windmills, rooftop gardens, Monarch milkweed stations, permaculture rings—fans of eco-resilience.

While mixed algorithms generate hurricanes, cyclones, and garbage gyres, psyche spins information clouds, mindstreams, teleodynamics. Hominization is a conscious force, bearing the signet of late-nineteenth century philosopher Charles Sanders Peirce who proposed, "By the pha-neron I mean the collective total of all that is in any way or in any sense present to the mind, quite regardless of whether it corresponds to any real thing or not."[13] Peirce's trope encompasses cave paintings, mud huts, castles, cities, theogonies, cosmologies, topologies—strata that weave mind and matter, climate and consciousness. In this ontology, a metaphor is no less mintable than a metal.

Teilhard called it *Le phénomène humain,* a klatch of sentiences exchanging all their tales and tidings. Hominids may suffocate and incinerate their gods, but there will be a corroboree and town hall before Armageddon. Every participating spirit will have its say, parrots and rhinos, lynxes and starfish too. Given shamanisms and sciences yet to come, mere apocalypse is a copout.

When the Sixteenth Karmapa, Rangjung Rigpe Dorje, was brought to drought-stricken northeastern Arizona in 1974, it hadn't rained for seventy-five straight days. Crops were dying. The Tibetan lama stepped from his vehicle and stood facing weather-beaten Hopi Chief Ned. As planned, the medicine man invited the Karmapa and his entourage into the kiva where they chanted, mostly the Karmapa did. Proto-Uto-Aztecan shifts in the rain call were realigned to Proto-Sino-Tibetan phonemes.

Afterward, the visitors parted in brief but warm formality. The car jounced on unpaved Four Corners highway, as the Karmapa began to recite a *puja,* a devotional prayer. Forty minutes later, as he raised his chant, the clear, blue cloudless sky darkened. A witness recalled the moment:

> I alternated between driving and watching, transfixed by something quite unbelievable, namely this stage-by-stage, magically time-enhanced transformation of a clear blue sky into a solid steel-gray-and-black-colored sky that was actually quite frightening to look at. It is challenging to behold such an intense level of concentrated, rapidly magnetized energy so suddenly made manifest from something seemingly empty.
>
> As the Karmapa brought the mantra back, there was enough vestigial correspondence left for psychic correction. It was the Hopis who made the rain, but it was the Karmapa who reconciled the notes. He made the right sound, set its pitch and chakra color, and it was deep enough and wise enough to be real.[14]

Deep enough and wise enough to bring rain . . .

TWO

Genome

CELLS

The circle is a primal archetype. The curvature of space-time under gravity causes planets to be round, to rotate in place, and orbit stars. It likewise causes stars to be spherical, electrons to orbit atomic nuclei, and particles to develop spin as well as charge. Life on spheroidal planets develops as curled membranes in waveforms in tides, pools, and tidepools. These nascent live spheres seek space (breathing and nourishing room) while developing metabolism and mechanism within the fractal constraints of their evolving masses and themes.

Gastrulation is the transformation of a single-layered hollow blastula (inherently a rounded epithelial sheet of cells) into a multilayered, scrolled template for beings from mosses and worms to mice and giraffes. It is a series of taut round dances under a spell of stones. The threader of these minute gemstones is a wireless loop connecting cosmic stations, transmitting paired helices that deliver interdimensional messages as "shape" seeds; in other words, DNA is a clear channel across zones of manifestation. Everywhere, creatures and landscapes are doing its tangos and twists of becoming.

Life is a module, made up of other modules, each inside each other without reference to what they are collectively inside of. Bodies are melds of bacteria, viruses, and other micro-creatures with their own cosmoses and skies. In a pre-Cambrian epoch, many small curvatures—cylindrical, octagonal, hexagonal, tubular, granular, snaky, striated, conical—collaborated on a community, the prototype cell. They shared their geometries, quantum states, spins, talents, and molecular numbers to form a compound entity. Billions of them basted their bustling metropolis inside semi-porous membranes.

Once allied in more perfect unions, cells coalesced into colonies, forming a variety of multi-cell prototypes—molds, fungi, algae, foraminifera, radiolaria: microsporidia, liverworts, rotifers, polyzoa. Some of their forerunners annealed into jellyfish-like, clam-like, and wormlike colossuses, layers of tissues ballooning as organs: creatures inside creatures inside other creatures—precursors of plant and animal kingdoms.

Don't forget: the cells of our body are independent life forms that became co-dependent to transmit a source code. Our personal identities require their continued cohesion, cooperation, and cloning. They listen, in their way, to our silences, sublimations, and thoughtforms.

It makes no sense—yet not only "here it is": black-feathered birds that "know what they know and can ponder the content of their own minds."[1] Reality is too big to be framed by meaning, yet too endemic to mean anything else.

Life on Earth began as a metabolizing autogene. Once it proved its chemistry—that it could breathe and digest—it spread pandemically, waking sea minerals from the dreamless satori of matter. Biological transmutation is the core of the system: inanimate molecules animated. Reveille recurs in each organism at the maturation of its sex cells, repeating the rite of passage and recruiting fresh molecules into living cells.

In the paragons of anthroposophy, plants and animals reenact nostalgias from prior worlds on other planes, culminations of Lemurian and Atlantean epochs and their transmigrations.

Zooids on Earth dwell now in twin environments—cell and planet—each with its membrane, niches, prey, predators, and climate. The first Dutch microscopists were astonished to find whole miniature bestiaries—schools, plazas, and assembly lines—through their glass. The "old" ones dwell inside each cell, while their consortia explore the next layer of creation. Each in their way, cells and creatures engage currents, storms, and temperature regimes. Subcellular and multicellular agendas ramify generationally, converting microbiomes into biomes—greenhouses into ecospheres—though either must cobble and fight its way there.

The world inside a cell membrane is run by its own microdynamics and weather—nucleation, unstable saturation, macromolecular phase shifts—as well as by structural fields of microtubules, microfilaments, and cytoskeletons, plus the activity of microbiota and so-called "junk DNA" (noncoding sequences within the same organism).[2]

Acts from which chordates derive pleasure were deemed invasive by free-living cells—life forms do not like being penetrated, especially at their outer membranes; yet they submit willingly to eros. It came about this way: Presexual colonies were innately cannibalistic; proto-organelles indiscriminately devoured each other. Some predators got trapped alive in their prey's membranes. Having to make sense of the dilemma, they decided, in a chemico-tactile sort of way, that life was happier inside than out. They stayed. Preying became prayer—fertility.

"In the earliest animals," proposed archaeo-biologist Lynn Margulis, "reproduction became enslaved, imprisoned by sexuality. The associated spirochetes* developed permanent attachments to their hosts. . . . The elaborate processing of nucleic acids, the large ribosomes, and the incessant internal activity of eukaryotes† behave as products of composite ancestry."[3]

Crossbreeding accelerated evolution. The cell became the original melting pot, as DNA exchange—dating—replaced solitary cloning. Design got transmitted microbially; traits were replicated by the RNA of their lovers rather than their own. Somatic therapist Stanley Keleman named the event "sexuality, self, and survival." Those similes

---

*Spirochetes (or spirochaetes) are double-membraned, flagellated proto-bacteria.
†Eurkaryotes are animals made of cells that have nuclei enclosed in a nucleic envelope.

pack a wallop, as "s" is the last hinge between being and nothingness. Hermaphrodite sea stars and parrot fish conduct sexuality, self, and survival too.

Each genotype brought a repertoire of ancestral attributes; each phenotype expressed a permutation of their protein messages: "[T]he bacterial genetic system is global and has been for at least two billion years."[4]

Translation by amino acids (DNA) reflects a universal code. A fungus or virus or horse chestnut is written in the same nucleic acids as a mouse, hen, or hare—not just at the beginning but now, and forever. Ginkgos, flatworms, geraniums, and owls mix at nucleic levels without a biochemical blink: same code, different families or phyla—no Rosetta stone needed. The amino acids that transcribe acorns of valley oaks and tentacle rings of echinoderms dictate sphenoid bones of otters and pelvises of primates. They make berries, wax, silk, dams, nests, yurts.

Every creature on Gaia can be topologically and fractally converted into any other if dipped in the energy called time.

The Baphomet may be a chaos-magic androgyne, but it limns a sex-changing composite of plants, animals, and fungi. We were made not by *more* sophisticated lab technicians but by pagan zooids, tossing information arrantly, letting Darwin and the ethers do the rest. Commensalism underwrites life, from the minute-by-minute mitoses that restore our designs to the meioses of microbes that live in our tissues and transfer their RNA into the nuclei of our cells, triggering mutations and consequent speciation.

Sperm and egg tribes originated when a protozoon cleaved into a self-same pair and, marveling at a mirror that was not a mirror, vanished into multicellular life. We each contain a replica of that mirror, somewhere in the spool that connects us to pre-Cambrian dawn.

A spermatic bud is composed of primary organelles: carbon-based microtubules and microfilaments stacked in axonemes and other kits to form a sleek marine robot or metallic-like drone designed to perforate information systems and insert its data. The sperm's head of coiled chromatin fibers, surrounded by a flattened acrosome, resembles a computer-mouse-shaped worm stripped of free-living functions. Linked by two centrioles to a beating flagellum, it swims on expulsion in clan swarms toward an egg.[5] Every male thereafter, fishes to loons to prairie dogs and chimpanzees, reenacts its propulsive surge on both macro- and micro-levels—as eros, then as fertilization and embryo.

Gender was an afterthought, for courter and courted—semen and egg—remain identical at base. Each seed is a gender-fluid zooid bearing its syllabary on a grain. At syzygy, their DNA is exchanged, and a blastula forms, the matrix of every terrestrial organism. It starts as a single cell fusion with grunge from each of its progenitors, then divides: two, four, eight, sixteen, thirty-two, sixty-four, one-hundred-twenty-eight, two-hundred-fifty-six, five-hundred-twelve. When it has enough stem cells for multicellular expression it involutes—gastrulates—becoming the mold for a full Linnaean taxonomy, though from looking at a blastula, you couldn't tell a pigeon from a pig. In its Cambrian vestige, you couldn't tell a monkey from a rose bush.

Sponges to sea hares, squids to koalas, DNA reshuffles, tissues migrate, orifices change position, role, scale, convexity, concavity, and erogenous zone. Desire shapes cell masses through sensation, behavior, and acts, deriving life forms and lifestyles by courtships.[6]

An animal may exist in wood or dale, pond or bay, dune or forest, plaza or encampment, at treetop or sea bottom, but its organelles—a motley medley of tribes including trichocysts, lysosomes, mitochondria, and Golgi bodies—stay oceanic, gestating in their own waters. The microbiome develops in that membranous sea, an uninvited flotilla of bacteria, viruses, viromes (viral meta-genomes), fungi, algae, vestigial protists, archaea, prions—rogue proteins that were once independent creatures—as well as microbes and microbiota that are *still* independent (though captured and colonized), and all these critters' genes. The HERV (Human Endogenous Retrovirus) library of nonhuman DNA, much of it comprising antique diseases passed through thousands of generations, swims in the same collation and is updated regularly by viruses, viromes, and retroviruses. Its squires "exchange DNA promiscuously and participate in chemotactic networks with each other, inducing new morphologies."[7]

That orgasm is a primal mode of information exchange shows how ecstatic and urgent information is. "[S]exuality was a preadaptation for tissue differentiation; cannibalism followed by indigestion . . . [and was also] a preadaptation for meiotic sex"—the halving of DNA codes for sharing data.[8] Because acts of incomplete cell cannibalism risk dystopic chimeras, meiotic reduction allowed resilience and variety while canceling extra toes, eyes, claws, stamens. Giantism, dwarfism, and fatal atavisms were averted on the mainline.

Though we are beasts of many nations by now—quadrillions of meioses and mitoses removed from our source seeds—pre-Cambrian looms continue to rebuild our body-minds from billion-year-old programming. Every millisecond, our genome, epigenetic field, and microbiome re-transcribe organelles, cells, tissues, and organs. They regenerate us through psi fields too—meridians and nadis, Rivers of Splendor sluiced by Chinese and Indian herbalists and acupuncturists, Jin Shin and eurythmic choreographers. If it weren't for the ongoing transmission of nucleic acids and *prana* reconstituting our organism from cardinal code every seven-or-so years, our span would not get much past crawling babes. Our survival is as fragile as a filament or codon and as resilient as a biodynamic field. The triage of the embryogenic doctor and her inner physician out-tilts all of biotech and the medical industrial complex.

MICROBIOMES

The microbiome is the hardware on which DNA builds and runs its software. The still-accessible part of that database is a frizzy hairball atop a plump globule of information spun by billions of years and yarns of evolutionary discourse during which the strings of primal organisms got wrapped in strands of their successors inside each other like shmoos. The yield is a fractally cached zip file of helical threads. The pearls (information) on the threads have been abbreviated, synopsized, elided, and recoded trillions of times, as mutations under incremental feedback encounter constraints imposed by prior and emergent systems. Though effects are organized randomly, each organism becomes anchor and compass for the next. The developing embryo doesn't have to know where it or its map comes from, the plan is already there—though an embryo unzips it in context.

If transported to Mars, a blastula would develop quite differently from on Gaia. Epigenesis requires genes, but genes don't express themselves without a planetary as well as a cellular membrane. Both sheaths interact with the unstructured blastula to develop extragenetically as well as genetically—from its own self-organizing properties and proteins as well as from exposition of its genetic inheritance.[9]

Epigenesis is what the biotech industry with its trait-bearing strands, bacterial edits, and spygate stop digits overlooks. The problems with releasing artificial pigs, salmon, tomatoes, and adenoviruses into the biosphere won't be known until long after Monsanto Jones* spills into corporate melds of Blackwater and Nestle.

As noted, life has an Etheric element too, for who could imagine all the instructions for making a beetle or chipmunk written in the exact right order on a micro-tablet—you can't misplace a codon? Neo-Darwinian science may dismiss teleodynamic resonance and permanent seeds in haste to post its own blueprint on the universe, but DNA remains sacred as well as secular—telekinetic as well as kinetic.

Despite their merger into the behemoths that tromp about these days, single-celled creatures retain primordial autonomy. They conduct their own communities and ecospheres, oblivious to our tomfoolery. Untaught by latter-day taxonomies, they go about procreating, mingling, prowling, breeding, spreading RNA across species, phyla, and kingdoms. Templars of their own I Ching, they diversify and reinvent life in amino-acid handshakes, matchmakers on their own terms.

COVID-19 is merely the most recent Graecian to invade Troy and kidnap its queen.[10]

I asked Continuum therapist Barbara Karlsen, whose book I am overseeing, for a snapshot of the microbiome informed by her starting point: cellular fluidity under somatic palpation.

---

*Check out "Monsanto Jones" on iTunes; in my song file it falls between "Mona Lisa" and "Monster Mash."

Continuum is a healing system developed by avant-garde dancer Emilie Conrad, using micromovements to restore tissue resilience, embryogenic intelligence, and evolutionary potential. Practitioners reactivate an innate epigenetic process, in part, by refining attention while visualizing ancestral shapes. By the principles of Continuum, break dancers, *chi gung* masters, jugglers, acrobats born without limbs, skateboarders, gymnasts, and children balancing alternately on multiple spheres all display vestiges of ancient cell and invertebrate resilience as well as precursors of superpowers.

Try softening into a sashaying sperm or receptive ovum, then a cavernous archenteron (a digestive and respiratory gut). Gastrulate into a hip-hop dancer, a snail crawling peristaltically up a chair or couch, a sea cucumber opening from a notochord, an octopus wriggling around corners. Simulate a lungfish sashaying along its carpet into life on land, then a descendant leopard prowling about furniture.

As an ardent practitioner of Conrad's system, Barbara pinged back, "I'm going through a spiritual awakening and emergence as I write!"

[T]he human body is host to various microorganisms including viruses, that have evolved to thrive in virtually any terrestrial or marine environment—scientists identify over 140,000 virus species in the human gut, half of which are new to them. . . .

We are one molecular being. One molecular creature . . . or one crystalline body of being and becoming that is more than human . . . it is planetary! It depends on how expansive you want to go with your molecular understanding. We can go from limited human dualistic understanding to include all molecular life forms on the planet, including viruses, mushrooms, adaptogen herbs, ecosystems . . . angels, elementals, etc., the whole organization of what we understand to be a planetary body. A planetary body that is really a molecular creature. . . .

[W]e are starting to appreciate the breadth of their vast intelligence: continuous transmutation, symbiotic assemblages, motility, ability to break down toxins, and complex architectural formations in the form of biofilms. Ironically, these microbes provide us with everything we need to survive the environmental challenges we now face. . . .

Just as mitochondria (bacteria which survived caustic environments) evolved in our human cells for respiration, we too may be on the verge of a whole new evolutionary leap. That said, we must do all we can to prepare our biological terrain to receive it. Just as a leap of faith takes a certain amount of courage, an ontological leap requires a whole new biological terrain.

Instead of making microbes the villains, maybe we should see them as the harbingers of important genetic upgrades, genetic upgrades that are now essential for our human survival on a toxic and dying planet. In this sense, the [COVID-19] pandemic has already re-shaped us as it intensifies the transparency between humans and microbes, rearranging the very strata upon which our present human existence stands or falls. . . . [W]e are redefining what it means to be a human dwelling on the Earth.[11]

I next asked naturalist Darin De Stefano for his version of the microbiome:

In the microfloral ecosystems of our bodies—inside and outside— animals, and we humans particularly, can be intelligently understood as a community organism whose staggering cellular diversity is the primary platform of our health and intelligence. 50+ percent of that diversity is and must be bacterial.

We are an animal who only arises from and within a swarming bacterial soup—almost as if we, the animals, are a peculiar expression of bacterial evolution and, I believe one could argue, intention. For within our bodies their communal powers achieve astronomical magnification. They become human with us, and we cannot become human without them. This is what it means, at a cellular level, to be human.

The relationship is not cause and effect, as too often presented by science. No. It is *identity*. We are *the same creature*.[12]

Within each genome, natural immunity and the vital body play uncredited roles in maintaining homeostasis until they don't. Then a novel coronavirus becomes a pandemic. In my condensation of physician Zack Bush's "understory," viruses and retroviruses transport fresh RNA between organisms, functioning as a natural genetic updating and innovating machine. Without mutating viruses—and perhaps pre-organic amino acids from space debris—our cells would never have developed stem pluripotency or evolutionary potential. Mammals have interpolated RNA from jellyfish, fungi, willows, oaks, insects, spiders, plankton, club mosses, snails, as well as comets and meteorites. Alleles jumping species and phyla led to differentiation of the original blastula and its riots of fungi, plants, and varmints on Gaia. Fragments of Callistan, Martian, and Europan life, if there be any, must also have infiltrated our genome along the way.

Our collective microbiome runs this diverse ecosystem software, functioning antithetically as mutagen and antigen—orgy and chaperone. Without viruses constantly interfering in jellyfish, lungfish, amphibian, and reptile evolution, there would be no birds, mammals, primates, or spiders.

We are viral and pandemic in our database. A virus knows that. Of course, it does. It might be the only thing it *knows*.

In their book on the microbiome, gastroenterologist Alessio Fasano and his coauthor Susie Flaherty write, "Our human genome has coevolved with trillions of constantly changing microorganisms found in and on the human body. . . . [W]e are the *product* of coevolution . . . with the metagenome (the gene array from our microbiome), which contains from 100 to 150 *times* more genes then we do"[13] (italics mine). That's nothing to sneeze at. These heedless prowlers get expressed according to diet, environment, and countless other cofactors. Long ago they subsidized differentiation of that volvox-like drifter into the entire ecosphere. That portends a more hopeful interpretation of the corona crisis than has generally been considered. In this reading, novel coronaviruses are common occurrences that respond to changes in the environment. COVID-19 didn't just come from bats. Bats were its vector, but it was a holistic response of the biosphere.

According to Bush, technogenesis has induced a new factor within a shuffle of biomes and microbiomes. COVID-19's RNA spike is a viral reading of pesticides from agricultural industries, notably Monsanto's Roundup with its life-killing glyphosate. Paraquats are evolutionary agents, as are antibiotics pumped into factory farms. Lake-size cesspools micturated by our cousin pigs transform surrounding biomes. Acres-long GMO farm-beds in synthetic soils and industrial fish farms—or fish "kills"—send their data to the microbiome. Bronchial passages may override a long disgorge of methane, carbon dioxide, industrial radiations, fossil-fuel exhaust, exotic metals, and particulate matter, but the viral layer is a finer reader of waste from combustion, computer and bit-coin industries, and pharmaceuticalized tap water. Like a t'ai chi master, it translates every molecular pat or strike into intelligence and response.

There is no net vast enough or fine enough to keep each of us out of the other's snare.

In this context, COVID-19 is a Gaia-protective response to ecumenical toxicity. Clumping with venoms, it runs more information through our microbiomes than they can handle. This overload, not the virus, says Bush, is what is making people sick and killing them. The hypoxia of COVID is not a *respiratory* symptom but cyanide poisoning of the blood in response to the climate crisis, molecular promiscuity, and the choking of planetary oxygen. The hyperinflammatory immune response or cytokine storm is triggered by frantic signaling among cells.

Yet, Bush assures, most of those infected have their RNA updated without serious harm. They receive regular COVID-19 updates—bit loads from the environment—and develop immunity. From his view, our species is responding to an altered planet by refreshing its database and evolving. To the microbiome, a novel virus is neutral information—and microbiomes are information gluttons.[14]

The pandemic is a bio-awakening or, at worst, a global healing crisis. The genetic message is itself an expression of a vaster wisdom, its cosmos-wide origination beyond any planet, solar system, or galaxy. Why do you think that those Roswell aliens, hypothetical or autopsied, bear twin helices too?

THREE
Dreamings

BUTTERFLY DREAMING

Imagine a physicist dreaming that he is conducting an ultimate experiment on the nature of matter. This is the one that will nail the boson to the bottom of the Cask: the so-called God particle. He attunes his oneiric microscope much as he would one of metals and glass. "What's the difference," his dream self avers, "if it is all a dream?"

Now he is standing beside a cyclotron smashing particles. He awaits a rogue rune to break the plane of the dream.

From a Freudian view, he is fulfilling wishes and fears from his personal ego, pinging the façades of his profession onto the cerebral cortex's xylophone where together they play a song of symbols.

No dream physics takes place or *can* take place.

If this is a lucid—self-aware—dream, then the physicist is exploring the epistemological basis of his empirical inquiry. Science is alchemical in both Paracelsian and Jungian senses, for the dreamer is excavating simultaneously: (1) matter; (2) the representations of matter in physics; (3) his own unconscious mercurial seeds; and (4) the paradoxical and transformative nature of unconscious representations. The more primal and cardinal the representations, the more seminal their aliases. That's the key to all transmutations—hermetic, shamanic, homeopathic, psychosymbolic, quantum-physical, proto-chemical, isotopic.

Perhaps the dreamer is an Astral traveler on a world that has not developed physics and built microscopes—a planet in this or another Milky Way. In its clair-oneiric dissemination across the universe, his dream turns into a technological act. He is using Bronze Age tools— only you wouldn't call it "bronze" there—to dowse the basis of matter *in a dream*. Because he and the bronze are archetypal, their isotopes can be melded across the multiverse and its periodic charts.

Now, remove the dreamer from his dream but not from the archetype. He is a smith conducting experiments with a forge and crucible. Eventually his civilization will discover lenses, and a descendant of his will work with mineral-based electron scopes and cyclotrons—my first dreamer returned.

I am leading us in a contrived circle because the attempt to source matter—to scoop its ontological basis—*is* a circle, *and also is taking place in a dream:* a waking dream, a phenomenology broadcast through microtubules.

Matter is physical, oneiric, alchemical, and epistemological: a cosmos, a dream, a thoughtform. Sentient beings are how matter thinks about matter—and there is no proof that it exists otherwise. And even if it does, there is no way for a dream of being a person, or a butterfly, to alight for certain on its own ontological plane.

At the butterfly house across the street from the Rosenberg castle in Copenhagen, so many winged caterpillars float that we visitors experience brief landings on our clothes, hair, hands. A sense of their world is conferred by touch. They say silently: "We alight, we like your colors too, we are not afraid of you. What do you think of us, big ones?"

Butterflies bring lightness, color, dance, surprise, but mostly lightness—large fluttering wings bearing illuminated wyrms.

According to a wall chart, about ten or so butterfly varieties dwell here, including the blue morpho, which is larger than the rest. On iridescent wings, its blueness glows. Wingspan gives these imagos a stabler gait in air than its mates, so morphos seem to glide, chasing in pairs and trios around us.

The chart attributes their iridescence to the fact that blue scares predators. A greater number of blue ones evaded bird meals.

A neo-Darwinian by upbringing, I accept this diagnosis but add a daub of "Paul Klee" blue: a Lemurian vibration. Blue is poison, but a fifth-chakra emission: clairvoyance. Its calibers of sunset—magenta, violet, mauve, indigo—transmit harmonies of psychic energy. Blue is yellow's antipode, the light that is reflected when yellow is absorbed. A lake is actually yellow, the sun blue. The colors on butterfly wings are not pigments but reflections of light off nano-molecular structures that excite the bluest of blues, blackest of blacks, and someday may make more efficient solar cells.

Four of the butterfly varieties are orange, identified on the chart as Julia, Postman, Tiger Wing, and East Mexican Banner. With the morphos, they glide in mute minuets of orange and blue. There are some flying yellows too, and others with transparent veined rings.

Take away a bit of white's Etheric luminosity, and what remains is yellow—golden as a crown, buttercups in a field, marsh marigolds, a finch's wing, tansy blossom, a plastic flute. The reasons that yellow exists are (1) white is too brilliant to be seen, so yellow is its filter and costume, revealing that first light has not only brightness but meaning and depth, and (2) yellow is what happens when a smaller, colder sphere intercepts the output of a star. Witness Gaian sunset, a fusion-clash of wavelengths at curvature's edge.

I do not feel bad for the butterflies captive in Copenhagen, though I imagined I would. Their zoo was planted with their favorite flowers and, if that wasn't sufficient, their hosts hung papyrus-thin strips of banana, orange, and watermelon from the ceiling. These surface-area wafers are centers of great clustering. Other delicacies are strewn in dirt around the plants. It is butterfly nirvana.[1] And they are only dreaming of being butterflies, as we are only dreaming of being butterfly-keepers.

A Chinese Taoist parable from around 300 BCE sets the terms: *Once upon a time, I, Zhuangzi, dreamt I was a butterfly, fluttering hither and thither. To all intents and purposes a butterfly, I was conscious only of my happiness as a butterfly, unaware that I was Zhuangzi. Soon*

I awakened, and there I was, veritably myself again. Now I do not know whether I was then a man dreaming I was a butterfly, or whether I am now a butterfly, dreaming I am a man.

ABORIGINAL DREAMINGS

When subjective cortical stimulation gives rise to credibly credulous narratives, the trances are called "dreams," though sensory input, particularly audio, can influence a dream secondarily.

Dreams unfold in the brain like scotomas of migraine auras. In the latter, blind spots, pulsating zigzags, and "Alice in Wonderland" character and landscape distortions occur as bursts from mostly the brainstem bombard the optical cortex.

Dreams, likewise, synapse in sensorimotor zones of the cortex, not in the sense organs whose modalities they impersonate.

The narratives of dreams are joint creations of conscious and unconscious elements of the mind, equally egoic and hermeneutic.

Nick Bottom's "past the wit of man to say what dream it was" is acknowledged cross-culturally but, like consciousness itself, it is subjective and existential. No one has seen or felt another's dream. Secondary artifacts alone testify, along with the oral and written literatures of dreaming. Somnambulism and dream speech extend to other animals' oneiric fugues, chirps, and barks. An electroencephalogram-trackable REM (rapid eye movement) is shared by birds and mammals.

Even cynics who consider dreams neural static of no consequence admit to their existence and to having them.

It is myopic to think of dreams as "just dreams." They are realities, as vast and complete as any other. A dreamer is a traveler.

Insomnia is a psychospiritual crisis—a resistance to crossing bardos as well as a disease of biorhythms and mind. Pharmaceuticals are bardos too.

The problem with sleep hygiene and its sleep doctors, sleep labs, and sleep drugs is that they force-feed a bardo shift. Some bardos are crossed only by the neurotransmitters of relaxed intention, for their barriers are neither incidental nor pathological.

* * *

The Australian Aboriginal set of practices to which Old English *drēam* (Dutch-German *droom*) has been applied is *not* a dream. It is an intersubjective trance, classified colonially by anthropologists and intercultural tourists. It is questionable whether there even is such a "Dreaming" apart from a sociological container for indigenous modes of belief and action. Aboriginal Dreamings are, more accurately, transgenerational pools of knowledge drawn from scientific and shamanic modes of perception.

Australia's native Dreamtime *includes* dreams and may be partially conferred in dreams, but it is more broadly enacted by telepathy and by extrasensory as well as sensory contact with stones, fungi, plants, animals, stars, bodies of water, runes—a group-based *scientia* transmitted orally.

At the same time, the "Dreaming" is a creative translation, or mistranslation, of the Aranda seme *alcheringa,* which is otherwise rendered as "the eternal, uncreated."[2] Some anthropologists have dismissed the *alcheringa* as a Western malaprop, a conflation of a primal theogony and an eternal being (from the root *altjira*), which are accessed by psychic trainings and in altered states of consciousness.

The phenomenology and paraphysics of Dreamtime-like spells *are* universal, while a literal *alcheringa* is indigenous to *terra Australis*—its Aboriginal mode of geomancy. The original custodians of the Australian outback—Koombanggary, Walleri, Yanga—while wielding the southern Indo edge of an Indo-European Weltanschauung, traveled to a subcontinental island by following astrogeography and cosmology. The Anglo nickname for Australia—Oz—plumbs a clipped simile-driven trope: great winds deliver souls to Dreamings, as local bardos shape their subsequent enactment. We are no longer in Kansas or Oklahoma, even those who are.

The Australian Dreaming does *not* cross cultures; it is endemic to a near-universal pan-Australian Aboriginal view of reality, passed down by Pama-Nyungan ancestors who left their proposed Indo-African genesis 50,000 or so years ago and, in diaspora, cultivated and studied the Dreamtime.

While all people, and even all creatures, receive the same environmental signals, each tribe interprets them through cultural lenses and ontological implications: they filter *out* as well as *in* information—erase as well as excavate landscapes.

A Westerner (or a person from another indigenous group) may learn the technology of the Aboriginal Dreaming, but they cannot cultivate its vibration without becoming a member of an Australian band. In that sense, the Aboriginal Dreaming can't be practiced globally. It is an indigenous initiation, prepared, cultivated, adorned, and embodied over thousands of generations of liaisons with environments and spirits; it cannot be unwound from origin and etiology—too big a spool, too much wool. As a living pupa, it operates in regard to landscapes, visions, and clan histories. And no hard line separates its ethnobotanical, ethnozoological, and ethnogeological trackings from their mediumship in relation to supernatural entities and realms. The Dreaming is both geographical and geomantic.

English travel writer and novelist Bruce Chatwin, who lived for a spell with First Nation Australians, portrayed their lives and worldviews in a 1987 mix of fiction and nonfiction, *The Songlines;* he singled out the songs of the Dreaming as central to its science, arising in a sort of call and response with the landscape—a mantra conducted clairaudiently with a tree, a rock, an animal, a path, a site, a body of water. The land sang back and, as it did, sang itself into existence. "Songlines" are what led tribes through jungles and across deserts and oceans. These migrations were preserved and reactivated in songs.

Other animals and plants do call and respond with the land too, so the whole of reality is sung into being, created and covered by songlines, pandas and porcupines as well as frogs and songbirds. Nor is it a matter of which came first, the songs or the land. They give rise to each other, a paradox with *no* bottom.

The ability of individual Aborigines to glean real-time information from their home bases—births, deaths, clan crises—while in the outback foraging, hunting, singing, and vision questing, is a specialty of the Australian Dreaming, though similar technologies are practiced worldwide. Aboriginal Dreamers have the telepathic equivalents of cell phones. Remote viewing can be taught—anything can—but its application cannot be exported from its cultural setting any more than a radio can turn on without an electrical cord and outlet or a battery.

Jane Roberts was the only person who channeled the multipersonal entity "Seth" because "it" appeared as Seth only when "speaking" through her field. Yet "Seth" has countless subpersonalities depending on who is channeling and on what world. Each superconscious source transmits through different planets, cultures, tribes, and creatures at their own frequencies.

Other psychics who may have channeled a "Sethian" source include Plato, Plotinus, John Milton, William Blake, and Milarepa. Alice Bailey probably channeled "Seth" under the name "the Tibetan." Contemporary psychic teacher John Friedlander, who sat with Roberts's group during her later mediumship, continues to channel the consciousness he encountered there under handles like Mataji, Yukteswar, and Babaji.

In that sense, the first settlers of Australia attuned to a unique Dreaming that has no equivalent in any other culture or practice. Their songlines and shamanic journeys may have affinities with what Indo-Europeans call astral projection, but the Dreamtime does not map onto the astral realm of Western theosophists and psychonauts. It has meta-astral aspects—a similar attunement achieved in a different range.

Perhaps the Dreaming functions in the West as a displaced astral and etheric axis, as Aborigines travel longitudinally across Indo-European—Vedic and theosophical—planes.

To explore a landscape's horizontal astral axis, don't try to "look" peripherally to your left or right but extend your focus outward while letting the shift be received as if the center of your attention were being unzipped and peeled along a hinge down your forehead through your third eye to your Adam's apple. Then direct it to the right or left by being receptive to deep right or left orientations rather than by referring to your own right and left sides.[3] Although it's a metaphorical stretch, you might imagine it as a torque between two optically anisotropic materials—the refractive index of a landscape depends on the polarization and propagation angle of its electromagnetic qua astral field.

According to Friedlander (from whom I learned this technique), Astral-One-Degree-Left contains fragments of probable worlds. Raise your viewing plane to a treble-like astral frequency while polarizing it from the left. Astrologer Ellias Lonsdale described a version of this:

> Things like dreams and music and ideas are far more substantial than you'd think, because they link us to the source realm that gives birth to all matter. Each time you draw forth from the deep well of your creativity, you co-create the universe. You set forces in motion that are the latter-day equivalent of stars and planets.[4]

In other words, songlines.

Astral-Two-Degrees-Left (a more polarized state) encounters an empty immensity, the formless void of Genesis before the Big Bang.[5]

Astral-One-Degree-Right (propagated the other way) is the frequency of nonhuman animal consciousnesses.[6] Between us and each creature is a rune that binds us both together and apart. Our human identity may have been established during the Pleistocene by shifting a hominid axis to the astral left, achieving a *sapiens* perceptual range. The ancestors of the Oz Aborigines may not have shifted as much to the left or attuned to a different "left."

An element of the Aboriginal Dreaming is its cultivation of animals spiritually married to a clan or group. Members of a particular Dreaming telepathically align with its totem's nonhuman experiences. The Kangaroo Dreaming encompasses the natural and social landscape inhabited by nose-bumping 'roo mobs. The Emu Dreaming has a foraging, dust-bathing, flightless energy. The Echidna Dreaming transmits slow curling-into-a-ball ant-eating. Shark Dreamings plunge the oceanic deep. Opossum and Badger Dreamings scavenge "the bright."

A lineage, medicine society, or individual can "own" a specific Dreaming—to the degree that a non-capitalistic group can "own" anything, let alone something sacred and vast. In actor Baykali Ganambarr's portrayal of his character, a tracker named Billy in the 2018 Australian film *The Nightingale* set in an 1825 Tasmanian penal colony, he performs his Blackbird clan Dreaming by chanting a blackbird superpower boast, flapping his arms, dancing with zany leaps and, later, dispatching a high-flying blackbird guide for his female convict boss-lady. This is how Dreamings give rise to trackers and technologies.

If you receive input one notch more to the Astral Right, you enter plant and mineral consciousnesses that provide unique spirit shapes and medicines. If you shift farther to the right, you contact winds and storm systems, a frequency that weather-workers and sailors train.[7]

There are also Rock Dreamings, Tree Dreamings, Cloud Dreamings, and Dreamings associated with energetic outcroppings like Uluru: the colonizers' Ayers Rock.

Dreaming-like clairsentience crosses into the denser Physical-Etheric plane. We are ordinarily aware of only the plane's solid aspects, but Etheric subplanes mediate between Astral mists and congealed landscapes.

Leave the Astral by reducing your psychic frequency into a bass range. Cross from the polarized turbulence of the lower Astral into the smooth-spiraling lava of the mid-Etheric.

Etheric-One-Degree-Right is the staging area for conventional dreams, where the next day's and future realities are incubated in permanent seeds from the Buddhic plane of synchronicity and pure consciousness.[8] There, karma is summarized, focalized, and transmitted so that individual histories are coordinated and sewn together as lifetimes and worlds.

Etheric-One-Degree-Left intersects worlds in which we share parallel lifetimes.[9]

Etheric-Two-Degrees-Left is where the energy behind physical reality is propagated—a domain beyond birth, death, and the creation and destruction of universes.[10]

Artist and translator Robert Lawlor, drawing on both personal experiences and anthropological literature, provides one of the fullest outsider pictures of an orally transmitted Aboriginal encyclopedia. While honoring the Dreaming as a relic of an original Stone Age religion, he invokes it as active cosmogony, much like Chatwin's songlines, connecting the deeds of tribes to the formation of their landscapes. What modern civilization has lost, Lawlor says, is its engagement with inter-dimensional geography. He wonders:

> What has become of the vision of the physical world as manifestation of the invisible? What has obliterated the image of a whole and unified creation from the mind of humanity? Is the eternal Dreaming still present, hidden beneath the facts, theories, and fantasies of our present awareness?
>
> The Aborigines speak of the beginning of a creative epoch when world-shaping influences pervaded the universe, before its material formation. Every culture possesses creation myths, and all creation myths—from the Aboriginal Dreamtime to the story of Genesis to the big-bang theory—postulate an energetic phase prior to the appearance of matter and life. . . .
>
> In the Dreamtime creation, the ancestors' travels, skirmishes, hunts, assaults, and lovemaking scored the earth's surface, leaving their imprints in the earth's topography. In our scientific view, the earth evolved through a phase in which powerful geological and climatic forces shaped the earth's surface, raising mountains, creating oceans, carving river-beds, and forming rocks and deserts. The major difference is that our cosmology acknowledges only physical forces and Aborigines attribute consciousness to the creative forces and everything in creation. . . .
>
> [T]he Ancestors transferred their vibratory potency into the hills, creeks, lakes, and trees and then departed, diving into the earth and rising into the sky. The stage was now set for the physical emergence of the tribes, the plants, and the animals. From then on, the entire cosmos is continually revitalized by the primal potency flowing between the great Ancestors of creation: the unconscious and the conscious, earth and heaven, the All-Mother and the All-Father. . . .
>
> [A]s the Dreamtime unfolds, the mighty acts of the great Ancestors—their pains and joys, successes and failures, blindness and revelations—sculpt the earth. These acts are retained as a memory, as a world-shaping code. . . . The earth, then, is the love- and battle-strewn trysting ground of the Ancestors, undulated and

saturated with blood and semen from the virginal, wild, ecstatic union of the boundless universal Dreaming with the name-giving power of the seed.[11]

If that isn't complicated enough, the Dreamtime is a morality play, an origin tale executed by ceremonies and chants, an Eleusinian-like rite of passage, a coming-of-age vision quest involving quartz-crystal energy, and a death-and-regeneration cycle.

Once an Australian placeholder entered international pop culture, it enveloped a range of oneiric arts while spawning syntheses in what University of Sydney professor of religion Tony Swain called a "self-fulfilling academic prophecy."[12] By now, the term "Dreaming" has been so widely adapted and retooled that most cultures recognize both its indigenous Aboriginal iconography and mimic *alcheringas*.

In this book, I am using the Dreaming to address recombinant sets of Aboriginal hermeneutics and cosmology in the context of Western cosmology, avant-garde art, chaos magic, and what the twentieth-century poet Charles Olson called "causal mythology," meaning our imaginal participation in cosmos-creation. Avant-garde artists apply the term "Dreaming" to certain dance and operatic performances: mixtures of walkabouts, nonlinear dramas, "Tanztheaters," and choreographies of music, sound, performance art, and balletics. Each of these encompasses mythology, alchemy, vision quest, songlines, and a clairsentient view of civilization as a waking, machine-infested dream.

OCTOPUS AND CROW DREAMINGS

Creatures who share Gaia with us are souls too, living the same Dreamtime, wandering in its samsara, learning constraints and wonders of new bodies. Whales, elephants, owls, moles, skinks, and seals all have wisdoms, things to tell the universe, their gods, and us. We receive these gifts through their Dreamings and folkways. Otherwise, we are cooped, lonely beings in separate worlds.

While passing a pet shop advertising a new litter of hamsters in felt-pen scrawl on window cardboard, I wondered, where do they all come from? The shop didn't invent hamsters, though it might have bred them. For that matter, how do flies arise around a dead crab? Who are they?

If we all suddenly entered the astral field together, our hawk and salmon neighbors—even our mosquito and sow-bug neighbors—would look much like our human ones: autonomous souls. Remove karmically imposed costumes, and we are the same beings, sparks from the same Divine Will.

There is a reason that elephants attend funerals and memorial services, both elephant and human—*they remember.*

Octopuses and crows are, respectively, the most intelligent and talky invertebrates and birds. An octopus is a huge, highly evolved oyster with centers of intelligence and problem-solving coordinated in suckers along each of its eight arms, all reporting to a central ganglion. It is not an octo-pussie, it is an octo-hemispheric ganglion—a different branch of intelligence from anything else in the mammal class or vertebrate sub-phylum. It is more akin to a dweller in a Jovian sea, though Jupiter's and Neptune's "cephalopods" would have to be far more humongous to diffuse greater gravity, with bronchial cells evolved for methane metabolism.

In 2021, the United Kingdom recognized the invertebrate mind, adding an amendment to its Animal Welfare Sentience Bill, designating octopuses, crabs, squids, and lobsters along with "all other decapod crustaceans and cephalopod molluscs" as conscious beings.

Earth's eight-tentacled, shell-less mollusks shapeshift in sensitive chaos and nonequilibrium flux, as they squeeze their whole bodies and arms into and through narrow rock and shell openings and researchers' traps, finding the lone gap that matches their and the obstacle's topology. They also figure out how to unscrew a jar containing a crab.

They rocket from hiding places with such sudden acceleration, sustained speed, stealth, and shape- and color-shifting that they jump probabilities. This is what modern dancers and Continuum practitioners attempt with hominid bodies: genomic fluidity, embryogenic pluripotency.

Some observers have suggested that cephalopods are not just overgrown Darwinian oysters but mutants of meteor-riding amino acids that splashed down from somewhere like the Sirius system or Pleiades and attached their strands to the genome of a Cambrian gastropod, conferring talents of elsewhere.

Other meteorite RNA could have hatched the fungal kingdom with its subterranean networks and entheogenic vistas by splicing alien codes into a proto-seaweed or haploid hornwort spore. Fiber-optic-like root languages may be native to many stellar systems.

Mushroom enthusiasts have proposed that mycology contains the E.T. talents and terms needed for solving our eco-crisis, delivered free from the stars: environmental clean-up (turning oil and gasoline waste into gardens of bee-gathering flowers); natural batteries (storing and releasing electrical charge); miracle medicines (cleaning cells and clearing malignancies); living machines (running factories, Teslas, and space stations); mortuary cycles (replacing crematory ash with topsoil); plus non-photosynthetic respiration, vegan cuisine, jazz and Bach-like madrigals (when electrodes are attached to their seeding bodies, unique melodies for different mushrooms)—and shamanic travels, interdimensional intelligence, attunement to Divine Love, voyeurism of Unity Consciousness, and acceptance of spirits and death.

Cephalopods inspire their own exobiological speculation. Though they didn't fly here in saucer aquariums, their instructions might have ridden on comet cocoons:

> "With a few notable exceptions, the octopus basically has a typical invertebrate genome that's just been completely rearranged, like it's been put in a blender and mixed," said Caroline Albertin, marine biologist at the University of Chicago. "This leads to genes being placed in new genomic environments with different regulatory elements and was an entirely unexpected find."
>
> Another interesting feature of this aquatic wonder is its ability to perfectly blend in with the surroundings. This chameleonic behavior is triggered by six protein genes named "reflectins" which impact the way light reflects off the octopus' skin, thus turning it into assorted patterns and textures that camouflage the octopus. . . .
>
> These creatures evolved over a period of over 500 million years

and are known to inhabit almost every body of water at nearly any depth. . . . With all this "out of this world" evidence at hand, it's hard not to see the otherworldly traits of octopuses, especially their ability to redesign their DNA for a flawless life experience and extreme survivability. Could this be just a complex and misunderstood evolutionary process? Or were these tentacled invertebrates brought to Earth from another place in the universe by some unknown civilization?[13]

The octopoid is more than a biomechanical projector of marine vistas; it conducts Husserlian phenomenology, Basquiat-like Neo-Expressionism, subaqueous neo-Platonism, and Yvonne Rainer choreography—all underwater with natural paints and textiles. Octopuses change their color-and-shape biomimicries, making themselves into effigies almost as realistic as anything brushed by Michelangelo or J. M. W. Turner. Their chromatophores paint in reds, blacks, and yellows; their deeper iridophores propriocept iridescent blues and greens. Deeper yet leucophores pearlesce as ambient whites while mirroring passing landscapes and objects. At the same time, the creature stretches sacs in its skin layers to replicate bands, stripes, and spots and uses papillae to form ridges and bumps. Cuttlefish propose cephalopod ontology by effort-shape dynamics: dazzles of hue- and shapeshifting, hiding and reappearing in tactics of you-see-me-now, you-saw-me-then.

Works of molluscan body art generate credible rocks, kelp, other sea plants, black-and-white poisonous snakes, ocean bottom, even exotic paintings substituted for landscapes by scientists. The octopus faithfully turns into a rock or a fish or even a Miró. Mimicries are produced in instantaneous sequences, for its "critics" are onlooking predators, killer sharks and oversize groupers who render life-or-death verdicts.

Octopuses can make 150 to 200 such works of art in an hour!

In their diffuse eight-point intelligence, these chordates are more like collectives than any other sentient Gaian creatures. They speak to the myriad emanations of DNA wisdom. As the octopus rendition of the "Man from Galilee" goes, *put your hand in the hand of the hand of the hand of the hand . . .*

That is my way of saying that deeper sources of psi, precognition, telekinesis, and cell talk on this world go substantially unexplored.

Octopuses read the ocean and their own cell banks as they fluctuate and dart like underwater dervishes. Who knows what gods an octopus honors, what spirits she prays to, what *tonglens* she transmits through wounded seas.

Note, too, that, despite my invocation of a generic "octopus," this is a wide-ranging clan, not a circus performer from *Bozo under the Sea*. There are as many octopuses as there are morphs and masks of mollusk protoplasm, with new ones still being discovered; for all we know, octopuses invent "octopuses" by the hour.

"Octopus" is otherwise a class: Cephalopoda. Its over 300 known species include nautilus, Atlantic pygmy, hammer, dumbo, southern blue-ringed, East Pacific red, as well as those hidden from our semiology in the deeper deep. Within a basic octo-limbed, decentralized oyster template, they encompass a variety of shapes, gowns, color displays, iridescences, sizes (capped by the great Antarctic squid), bioluminescences (the blue glowing coconut octopus among the most psychedelic).

Octopuses and a few squid and cuttlefish species "routinely edit their RNA sequences to adapt to their environment."

> When such an edit happens, it can change how the proteins work, allowing the organism to fine-tune its genetic information without actually undergoing any genetic mutations. But most organisms don't really bother with this method, as it's messy and causes problems more often that solving them.
>
> Researchers discovered that the common squid has edited more than 60 percent of RNA in its nervous system. Those edits essentially changed its brain physiology, presumably to adapt to various temperature conditions in the ocean.
>
> DNA sequences were thought to exactly correspond with the sequence of amino acids in the resulting protein. However, it is now known that processes called RNA editing can change the nucleotide sequence of the mRNA molecules after they have been transcribed

from the DNA. One such editing process, called A-to-I editing, alters the "A" nucleotide so that the translation machinery reads it as a "G" nucleotide instead. In some—but not all—cases, this event will change, or "recode," the amino acid encoded by this stretch of mRNA, which may change how the protein behaves. This ability to create a range of proteins from a single DNA sequence could help organisms to evolve new traits.

[H]igh levels of RNA editing is not generally a molluscan thing; it's an invention of the coleoid cephalopods.[14]

This natural CRISPR science makes it seem that cephalopods have mastered clustered regularly interspaced short palindromic repeats. But is it a native outgrowth or an interplanetary splice? Psi-like "cell talk" or a suppressed chordate superpower? An axolotl-like specialty or a teachable rain dance? If biodynamic fields are fluid, shape-changing, and conduct epigenetic information, why eschew native resilience for commodity biotech?

The 2020 movie *My Octopus Teacher* has touched viewers in the way a flash drive from a trip to the Saturnian system, planet or moons, might: a visit with aliens whom we never knew (but with whom we share a solar system). Pippa Ehrlich and James Reed's documentary transcends prior cartoons, tropes, and sushi. Diver Craig Foster befriends a female *Octopus vulgaris* in his local South African kelp forest. For the better part of a year, they swim together, do contact improv, and even kiss arms (octopus says hello, sucker by sucker, alien to hominid, E.T. to Elliott). They dance and play hide-and-seek with schools of fish. This makes Tako nigiri cannibalistic.

With its suckers, each tentacle-full bearing a rudimentary mind, mother octopus swiftly gathers a hundred or so shells around herself as shark protection and sits on ocean bottom like a lady's fancy hat. As that hat, she rides the shark, the safest perch for a rodeo queen. She is a shell-covered changeling clown, as she masters her vertebrate predator. In a hypothetical Walt Disney version, hungry shark says, "W-w-w-here did that p-p-p-pesky oyster go?"

"Look on your back, bub!"

Foster remarks that his "friend" is more fundamentally intelligent than he is, for she is a giant underwater ganglion sprouting over hundreds of millions of years.

When a shark bites off one of her arms, she convalesces for a while, deep in her small shell-and-kelp stone cave, foreshadowing Steven Spielberg's E.T. There she grows a miniature arm that becomes a full-fledged tentacle. She jets about reborn.[15]

Octopuses have very short lives, proving that time, wisdom, and experience are nonlinear. Foster mourns the death of his young friend, who is old to herself, as she transfers her tidal lease and vital essence to her babes. She might well have flashed the words of Gautama Buddha: "I manifested in a dreamlike way to dreamlike beings and gave a dreamlike dharma, but in reality I never taught and never actually came."[16]

Crows are initiates by avian parameters, for they navigate mathematics of air and twig—no soft watery topologies for them. Conducting corvid algebra, geometrics, and geo-caching, they are grand empiricists and logicians, able to solve human-imposed puzzles involving different-sized pegs and a sequence of latches to get at food or drink. They can gauge, then beak-fill a beaker with tiny pebbles to raise its water level to their thirst.

Seventh-century Greek slave Aesop thought the "moral" for the fable "The Crow and the Pitcher" should be "Necessity is the Mother of Invention," but that anthropomorphizes and underrates its birds. With brain-hemisphere ratios that resemble our own, corvids were solving water puzzles seventeen million years ago when the only "pitchers" were eroded rocks and natural potholes and our ancestors were emerging from their shared ancestors with apes.

As humanity's shadow pets, these birds are well adapted to deforested suburbs and urban compost and decay. They understand a good cornfield, an overloaded truck, a litterbug picnic, a garbage transfer station, roadkill. Their talents include placing walnuts by car tires in traffic and retrieving the opened nuts at red lights.

A scarecrow in a field of corn is a relic of Neolithic magic, a stick sigil marking the boundary between human and bird.

Crows are not colorful like tanagers or toucans, but their tightly groomed feathers have an iridescent, satin sheen that contains the whole rainbow in the handsome way that old black-and-white films epitomize technicolor. They are among the most chromatic blacks I have seen. And their bodies are a perfect size, a compact avian doll. Neither eagle nor chickadee, they array, hop, pluck, and roost on rooftops and terraces with smug aplomb.

Crows and their close kin, ravens and magpies, don't sing like songbirds but speak High Crow, a birdtalk with morphophonemics, dialects, and tonal and volume ranges for manifold occasions, including the clicks, glottal stops, and tonal flutterings (purrs) that characterize some African and Native American languages. Linguists have identified a vocabulary of 230 High Crow words and counting. Crows can shift regional dialects like skilled actors or translators.

When you next hear big black birds cawing away on fences and rooftops or in the sylvan canopy or sky, don't think that they are trying out their vocal cords, making a racket for the sake of it or repeating themselves from bird-brained OCD. Those are proto-sentences, syntactic formations with vibratory and tonal nuances beyond our ken. Those crows are holding full conversations, informing each other about situations in corvid culture, entrepreneurship, metabolism, and ontology, while gathering hominid ethnology and ethnography, as behavior of humans sets their agency. They are saying, "Come here, check this out" or "Be careful, young chick. Hominids are undisciplined, unpredictable, dangerous, and, unlike crows, irrational." This is true even when, like the present author, they set treats on the lawn while keyboarding this page at a nearby table.

Corvid Crow is totemically related to "Crow," the language of the Apsáalooke tribe of Montana (with 2,480 speakers in the 1990 U.S. census). "Apsáalooke" translates into English as "children of the large-beaked bird." Human Crow is a Siouan-Catawban language family located in the Great Plains and Ohio and Mississippi valleys at the time of Euro contact.[17] Bird crows spread widely through a post-Columbian, post-Catawban landscape formed by European notions of manifest destiny.

A link between the two Apsáalooke was foreshadowed by French anthropologist Claude Lévi-Strauss who applied symbolic topology to myths and native taxonomies, turning birds, stars, and turtles into clan ancestors in pantheons that bridged the social and metonymic gap between nature and culture—the largest encodable yaw in our universe.[18]

Heckle and Jeckle, Walt Disney Studios' crows or magpies (1946–1981), exhibit the speech characteristics of their native manikins in mimicries of human vaudeville, as they squawk, "Ow! Ouch! It hurts! I give up," or "Never mind, old boy. I have a feeling our luck will change on this trip. I smell money," and "Wow, just what we need!" They even speak German, French, Japanese, and Albanian. With majestic corvid wit, they end one cartoon with, "I say we're safe. It's the end of the picture!"

To imagine what it is like to *be* a crow or raise a crow baby is not the same as to have a crow-size body, black feathers, and caw syllabary. Carlos Castaneda established this precept in his fictional or real shamanic dialogues with Yaqui brujo Don Juan Matus. To carry a crow's lightweight chassis in air and seek campsites, dumpsters, and run-over possums is a form of Tibetan *phowa* or astral transposition.

Crows and ravens do not like each other, though they share being corvids. The bigger turkey-tailed ravens have historically considered crow nestlings food: Old High German *(h)rabans* raid New Dutch *kraai* roosts—a deadly rebus for the blackbirds involved.

The enormous crow that just landed on a tree outside my window, shaking its branches, is both concretely material and an extension of its own mind. It wasn't always a bird and won't always be.

By the dependent origination of Buddhist ontology, the crow exists only because everything else that exists *exists*. It cannot be removed, absolutely or altogether, without its hole puncturing all of reality. The bird's stubborn persistence, stubborn to itself and to my view, is more trivial physically than psychically, but to put it that way misconstrues. The crow doesn't exist *either* only physically or psychically; those are interdependent.

That is, you can remove the physical bird from the universe more convincingly than you can remove the bird from consciousness—its own or mine—for those will go on using mind energy to generate new forms, none of them necessarily crows.

Magical practice is not to make the world magical or *more* magical. The natural world is magical enough. Magic is to guide people through manifestations—it guides porcupines and sea urchins too.

COVID DREAM ANIMALS

With the 2020 pandemic, we re-made our connections to the natural world. Like poems, these oracle cards are gnomic divinations at different frames of reference; see John Keats's nightingale, William Blake's tiger, John Donne's flea, Andrew Hudgins's swordfish, Mary Oliver's wild geese. Emily Dickinson's cat, Seamus Heaney's otter, Robert Kelly's ant, and countless other literary animals. Each arises where its frequency or sovereignty intersects human witnessing. Science is just another mode of divination.

Tardigrade

Tardigrades comprise a phylum of eight-legged segmented micro-animals, at most 1.5 millimeters in length. They were discovered under a microscope, swimming in microweeds in 1773 by German zoologist Johann August Ephraim Goeze who called them "little water bears." They have been dubbed "moss piglets" too.

Like hypothetical habitants of an ecozone below the ice of Europa or Enceladus, they are wormlike, crablike, grasshopperlike, with faces that suggest awe and agency.

A head with sensory bristles ravels into three body segments, each bearing a pair of unjointed legs, and a caudal segment with legs. Each foot has four to eight claws. The first three sets of legs are arched downward along the creature's sides, for paddling across tardigrade-scale seas (did you ever see a close-up of twelve ants on a gall-speckled boxwood leaf slurping away at a single water droplet landing from a higher leaf?). The fourth pair of tardigrade legs is directed backward and used primarily to grasp local substrates.

Tardigrades have no respiratory organs, so gas exchange is bodywide. Their gut is a bit of coelom at the gonads. A tubular mouth with gland-secreted stomatostyle teethlets—extensions of the shell—is used to pierce the cells of plants, algae, and tiny invertebrates, providing sip meals. After a short sucking pharynx and esophagus, most of the tardigrade is intestine, as the prime driver of the creature is digestion. A short rectum connects to a tiny anus.

Like lobsters, tardigrades shed their cuticle. Some tardigrades shit only when they molt, storing their feces in their shells.

The animal in action looks like a floating wombat or guinea pig in an oversized sagging tan suede wetsuit, its cuticle's sleeves and collar all but covering bird-like claws and face. Its expression is an optical illusion of folds with a cylindrical snouty mouth extruding: a black-and-white stylet-fanged vacuum nozzle made of microtubules.

Tardigrades have brains, a bilaterally symmetrical clump of ganglia and lobes made up of paired neuronal synapses. A single large ganglion connects the brain to the esophagus along a double ventral nerve cord extending to the anus, one ganglion per segment, lateral nerve fibers operating the limbs. Its thoughts, if you would consider them that, are primal hypnopompia. Its phenomenology is as timelessly gemlike as its being. It is that pair of complex insectlike rhabdomeric pigment-cup eyes that gets your attention—like the microbiome staring back.[19]

When bombarded by germicidal ultraviolet light, enough to kill any fellow microbe, a tardigrade glowed indigo-blue for fifteen minutes, then proceeded unfazed with its so-called life.

In future worlds of 6 and 7G, online meetings will be three-dimensional holographs. Participants can examine widgets, motherboards, and engines, and walk through each other's doppelgängers in virtual rooms. Magnified COVID-2030, its purple and pink spiked spheres floating like giant balloons, may be examined across the globe at the scale of a kidney or, for that matter, an automobile or galaxy. Cartoonists will depict tardigrades playing volleyball and croquet with spiked viruses.

My nine-year-old grandchild Hopper, the offspring of two indie film directors, bought a tardigrade NFT* (nonfungible token) and is

---

*A YouTube video of a basketball dunk or mobile op-art has become as negotiable as a fifty-dollar bill. Any artist or hacker can mint his or her own coinage, encrypt it, sell the code and password. No web surfer, filmmaker, or news outlet can view or show the video without purchasing its rights.

using its video to make a film about human-scale tardigrades who come from their planet in a saucer to rescue their tinier relatives from being trafficked through interplanetary space in rapt dormancy.

Tardigrades augur the next leap in software: programmable organisms. Hard drives will be made of salivary glands, medusoids (jellyfish larvae), and xenobots (frog stem cells). Memory will go as deep as biological time. Cells—microtubules, amino acids, proteins, carbon chains—will become the new computer memory, storing data far beyond the limits of inanimate silicon. Snips of messenger RNA from frog embryos portend not only the medicines but the laptops and smartphones of the future run by nucleic helices on qubits. The "cloud" will be stored in a tiny test tube. In principle, the entire database of the planet can be put on a stem-cell drive of a single frog egg.

Then tardigrades will collide with bears.

In 2021, scientists at the Nanyang Technological University in Singapore quantum-entangled hibernating tardigrades with superconducting qubits. They placed each frozen tardigrade between two capacitor plates of a superconductor circuit to form a quantum bit, or "qubit"—a unit of information. When the tardigrade contacted Qubit B, it shifted the qubit's resonant frequency. The tardigrade-qubit couple was then linked to nearby Qubit A. The qubits became entangled, and the frequency of the qubits and tardigrade changed in tandem, apparently making a three-part entangled system. Was the tardigrade truly quantum-entangled? If so, how does life respond to such a weirding?

One of three frozen tardigrades survived. It went on sleeping and dreaming of tardigrade things. It had already given fair warning: "I'm not part of your game. I don't come from where you do. You can't drown me, desiccate me, suffocate me, scald me, dehydrate me, bash me on the moon, and you also can't discombobulate me by quanta. I can shrink myself into a dehydrated ball and suspend my metabolism. You can put the database of your whole planet on me for all I care. I'll just go on error-correcting your intermediate-scale quantum information and dimensionally depleted artifacts."

Coyote

Furnace guy Lee Tubbs, a diffident Mainer, limned the eco-crisis while finishing with our balky firebox, then diverged, "Now coyotes—they're fierce S.O.B.s. When they want to eat, nothing stops 'em. There was one on my block, a big guy. I was out walking, and I saw a woman putting out her dogs. I told her, 'Better not. He's more than a match for both o' them if he's hungry.'

"She didn't know what I was talking about, so I pointed. She said, 'Oh, I didn't see him. Maybe that's why all the cats are gone missing.' Yeah, maybe!

"That coyote won't give in. Once he's made his decision, he'll go for it. He'll attack a moose. The moose can be kicking the fuck out of him, but he'll keep coming. There may be nothing left of a coyote, but as long as there's a jaw with teeth, it will keep biting and trying to feed."

I passed this story to my daughter Miranda in Los Angeles. She had her own *coyotl* report. She was out walking, talking to a friend on her cell, a facet of COVID evenings, when she heard a weird click-click-click. She looked around and saw an unfazed coyote, then realized that she was in a pack. They were on either side of her, an untold number in the dark. Her friend, knowledgeable about such encounters, said to keep moving, don't change your pace, don't look at them, and certainly don't run. After a while, the pack got ahead of her, and she detoured onto the front porch of a random house. She stayed there briefly because she realized the people inside were scarier than the coyotes.

Llama

Two llama antibody fragments uniquely block COVID's spike glycoproteins from binding to ACE2 receptors. During the Pennsylvanian subperiod of the late Carboniferous into mid-Triassic, our ancestors took leave of their common quadruped and departed in gait, diet, and songline. Now we turn back to our Eemian forebear, a four-inch long tree-climber who ate insects and worms, and request a microbiomic re-shuffle. We don't want the trail of a wooly domesticated camelid whose predecessors migrated from North America to Peru; we want the microbe it ate and converted out of Quechuan compost piles.

Crow

Murders of them dominate cities and villages (flocks of magician birds are called "murders"). They are talking the old tongue.

Humans dress as crows, in black hoodies, tights, gloves, and masks, try to "crow whisper." The crows look back, caw, and purr to each other, mocking and deciphering. They have something to say, a Dreaming to transmit, but without diplomacy more serious than Halloween costumes, we won't receive it.

My cousin in Southern California, not previously prone to psychic interaction, was visited regularly by the same audacious raven after her husband's death. "Jeff's looking after me," she said. "The grandchildren even call him grandpa." That is, Jeff's energy field and thoughtform had enlisted a bird or shape-changed into a raven-like spirit. It even showed up in the Dominican Republic when she went there on a cruise.

During an April 2020 phone conversation from coronavirus-ridden Berkeley, California, with spiritwalker Laura Aversano in the Bronx of New York, a very bold crow landed next to me.

Laura asked for an iPhone picture. I was too slow. She said, "He'll be back."

A day later, "Yes."

"Have you named him?"

Why, I wondered, would I do that?

Awaking in the middle of the night, it occurred to me, "The crow's name is obvious: CORVID."

Laura's email response:

"Wow . . . yes of course. Perfect name for perfect medicine. He is helping others to cross over but also issuing a warning, there will be more to come, the earth is destined to purify one way or the other, man is unfortunately making it worse. Crow is acting like a psychopomp. I can relate—Corvid the psychopomp, as is the wind this morning."

Rat

Herds of rats are running down the sidewalks of New Orleans with the abandon of buffalo or lizards on desert rocks. Chinese Year of the Rat: it's their city now.

Fly

A friend writes of sitting on her front porch in the sun, clipping her toenails and watching a fly wash itself for ten minutes.

The fly that landed on Mike Pence's forehead during the 2020 vice-presidential debate was espoused by the Left for casuistically shaming.

It is true that flies lay eggs in *merde,* and the black of a single fly highlighted the polar whiteness of Pence, in racial contrast and the 270-to-1 scale of hominid to insect.

My interpretation of that fly vis-à-vis the present situation is that our real agenda should be to find the same fly and interview it for *its* side. Not really, but that's the crisis we face. How do you begin to find, and contact-trace, it before and after, to get to the big picture?

When the fly leaves the set, it goes straight into reality, the one we are missing with our fixation on the sideshow where it briefly stopped. Our chance of finding it is roughly equal to our chance of stopping the melting of the glaciers or arising of mutant flies.

Go to around when that fly shared an ancestor with us, roughly 480 to 500 million years ago during the Ordovician, when arthropods went one way and our guys went another. Both left the Great Sea.

Elephant

Elephants, which share a relatively near ancestor with hippos and sea mammals, have a sense of self, greet one another with affectionate trunks, screams, group urination and defecation, recognize themselves in mirrors, decorate themselves with tiaras of clumps of grass, and speak at such low frequencies their "replica signals" can travel six miles through the ground and are heard through their feet. Nonhuman Rights Project attorney Steven Wise is currently seeking habeas corpus for an elephant named Happy who has been held for four decades by the Bronx Zoo Wildlife Conservation Society.

Pigeon

I am perched in a guest room in a Siena, Italy, monastery (September 2006). The world is almost black—dark magenta—and the sound, near and far, is of pigeons cooing on rooftops, an occasional metallic clank of something falling, hitting, and echoing, faraway.

As the curtain grows lighter, birds are taking flight, and the sound is of their wings. With each circuit of acrobatic flying, more pigeons join the flock, the rumble of beating wings getting louder and more drumlike, while the visual wave grows more complex: a billowing moiré.

Now there are hundreds of them, and their flight makes muted rhythmic thunder. As layers of birds awake and peel into the flock, the procession rises and falls, swoops and twists, turning left and right, deriving new variations on an overall sinusoid of what is no less than a communal dance to dawn.

These birds are praying, praying while flying, praying *by* flying.

The undulating stream is like no sunrise I have ever seen. It is intelligent, chaotic, cohesive. The wave thickens and complicates second by second, as more birds join. The air is littered with their falling feathers like flakes of a snowstorm, a few delicate crystals tumbling past me on the balcony.

Seven a.m. on the dot! A sudden clanging of bells builds to a deafening crescendo meeting the fortissimo of pigeons. Any birds that were still asleep join the circular prayer.

This is the climax of their parade. Thousands of them thunder in one ceremonial wave of two or three lesser sinusoids meeting and separating in elegant counterpoints. The sound is almost of a jet taking off. That so many can be aloft in a single, multidirectional pattern at the same time without bumping into one another is remarkable: an Olympic display of synchronized flying.

When the bells stop, the birds end their dance and roost, vanishing almost entirely except for a few enthusiastic stragglers in extracurricular circuits, ordinary avian flight about Siena. The clatter has settled too, becoming other species of fowl heralding sunrise by chirping in the distance, an occasional nearby coo.[20]

Fourteen years later, a hooded woman in black whirls in the Neapolitan zócalo like the ghost of a mariachi ballerina, a *danse macabre* to drive away viruses, vampires, and bats.

Bees

Bees conduct cross-species conversations in synesthesiac chords "con-fusing" color, taste, tactility, and sound. They are manufacturing sweets and serums, condiments in combs. On a boxwood tree, they sound like a band of Aborigines playing didgeridoos.

During our back-and-forth about time portals in the *Outlander* TV series, archaeoastronomer Ross Hamilton wrote:

> There is a place in Sunbright, Tennessee, on the side of a small mountain where a sound emanates sounding like a hive of giant bees. The Cherokee once buried their dead all around it, but no one has ever been able to get closer than fifty feet to it because it is terrifying to do so. I knew a man who saw and heard it, but I was never able to find it when I went for it. It was in *Ripley's Believe it Or Not.* More recently, an associate told me about a pile of singing (buzzing) rocks in Iroquois country.
>
> Apparently, one other buzzing stone was at Serpent Mound right in the center of the oval in the Serpent's mouth. It was a standing stone cut like a British menhir and nearly ten feet in height. The Late Woodland Indians or some early post-Revolutionary War farmer uprooted it and threw it over the eighty-foot cliff just adjacent. It is believed that these sacred places (and there were once many of them) were created to keep the ancient circuits alive with earth current for when the time comes to reactivate them.[21]

Octopus

Cephalopods have a lot to teach us: love, biomimicry, decentralized thought, multitasking, oogenesis, how to play with fish, self-sacrifice, stealth, shapeshifting.

Turtle

Up close the sea turtles on Poipu Beach in Kauai look older, more alien, and less friendly than from afar. Their expressions are beyond diffident, but I wouldn't deem them either aggravated or serene, though they have qualities of both. What they carry is not a human emotion; it is a mix of imperiousness, dignity, profundity, ferocity, knowledge. I don't mean that they are smart in a human sense, nor do I want to inflate them in anthropomorphic terms. But they are massively intelligent. Their wisdom is the wisdom of their species, their longevity and acquaintance daily with the sea and its mysteries, the crustaceans and codes that attach to their shells, as hieroglyphic as Herman Melville's whales.

Sea turtles' heads are like shaman masks. Their leathery necks and their movements of them suggest a model for E.T. Their breath as they surface, raising vertebrae out of the water, C6 and C7, is guttural and rude. It has an audible hiss that sounds like industrial steam or their cousins the snakes.

Herbalist Matthew Wood wrote me:

THERE IS A SACRED TURTLE GRAVEYARD AT THE BOTTOM OF THE OCEAN. NOBODY KNOWS WHY IT IS THERE: WHY THEY GO THERE TO DIE. IT IS A MYSTERY. THERE WILL BE MYSTERIES THAT WILL UNFOLD AS THE WORLD CHANGES. THEY WILL PENETRATE TO THE MARROW OF OUR BONES. IF WE ARE NOT READY, OUR BONES WILL BE SHATTERED.

When I asked Matt where this came from, he answered:

The statement above was made at the end of a pipe ceremony two years ago by my dear friend Susan Yerigan. This was the last great ceremony we had before a stroke left her speech deeply injured.

Then it struck me that we have already entered the Land of Mystery. No matter what else we say about it, COVID is a Mystery. It is almost like an opening initiation into the Unknown. Meanwhile, the cry of "fake news" so totally dominates the atmosphere that there is little certainty about anything. It is like humans are ripping apart their own nest. I cannot help but see this as the perfect platform for Mystery to continue its descent down to our bones.[22]

"Goodbye goodbye," says poet George Mattingly, "it seemed so real."[23]

FOUR
Meta-Sciences

FIELDS

Realities are deeper and more veridical than universes, for realities are phanerons (see Charles Sanders Peirce earlier), arising as phenomena in any world or present to any mind. A quantum underbelly totes a Newtonian universe because phanerons, as hybrids of mind and matter, jump thresholds, making rules as they go.

A classic physics of ping-pong balls, meteorites, and bullets delivered dependably from the time that Newton assayed and denominated it at the cusp of the seventeenth and eighteenth centuries CE until its bedrock dissolved into quarks, preons, and strings. Their emptiness and entanglement eliminated any concrete basis for the concrete.

In valorizing objectively oriented modes of inquiry, twentieth-century historians of science dismissed Newton the alchemist and Darwin the theologian, yet physicists ended up back in the briar patch, confronting Hermes and the Sphinx anew, as light, space-time, relativity, and biological transmutation.

When double-slit experiments at the turn of the twentieth century established tenets for subatomic behavior, physical reality was repealed—Aristotelian and Newtonian brands—and replaced by a ghost surrogate. Quantum mechanics operates more like dreams or hypnagogia than kilns and road repair.

At the heart of material manifestation, the distinction between a particle and a wave—between radiation as matter and radiation as energy—is as positional as antipasto and as mercurial as light. Because probabilities supplant clean outcomes, measurement is prorated according to what's measured and who holds the rod. Democritus's particles and the angels on Thomas Aquinas's pinhead proposed as much early in the game; it took another few centuries for scientists to realize that those angels *were* particles. We have not assimilated the radical implications, or we wouldn't still be waving the flag and saving the parade.

The universe we observe today, quasars to quarks, is what a Pangolin Dreaming of a universe might look like. Physicists and mathematicians can't solve an atomic quilt that comes into being only when—*or while*—they do. The witness can be a lizard or cow, as long as it churns out phanerons. Without "being," stuff vamooses in a wink. A blind moose turns the universe black.

From crop circles to UFOs to the memory of water, attention is trapped in liminality. Seekers anoint, trenchant skeptics refute—both ignoring what things *mean*.

We didn't see the left hook coming while we were mesmerized by the right jab.

While Alice's rabbit hole applies only to very, very, very tiny things, all systems are made of these, and that can *never* be incidental. We are how quarks and electrons personify and perform at bear and Bear Shaman levels. Intelligence, natural as well as artificial, uses qubits and uncertainty states to think anything, even bus fare. Newton used the same qubits without suspecting them. The theologian took over, for the physicist had no tools to trowel deeper.

"For all we know," sang Rosemary Clooney—Nat King Cole, Sarah Vaughan, Dinah Washington, Billie Holiday, and Kate Hudson at the 2020 NBA All-Star Game in honor of Kobe and Gianna Bryant—*"this may only be a dream . . ."* So yes, *"we come and go / like a ripple on a stream."*[1]

QUANTUM MECHANICS

The only way to resolve anomalies and paradoxes arising from quantum mechanics, as interpreted differentially by Max Planck, Werner

Heisenberg, Albert Einstein, and Niels Bohr, is to concede the primacy of consciousness. There is no competing or mislaid variable at the proper scale nor can anything else compass the ontological discontinuity. I'll come back to that verdict in chapter 7.

Formal reality is less a mirage than a dust-up of Cartesian duplicities that jump the shark of quantum uncertainty, giving worlds richness and dimensionality. Look at how numinous, meticulous, and gorgeous this reality is, let alone how astonishing that it exists at all, let alone so various, dignified, and vast . . . let alone—

Uncertainty is a greater gift than immortality, for no one wants to be bound to one script or cinema forever. For even the oldest tortoise or redwood, this is a limited engagement.

Lay cosmologist Sean McCleary proposed (in a short informal essay pasted into an out-of-the-blue email to me) that the evolutionary event that took place 13.8 billion years ago was a combination of two frequencies, consciousness and matter, but "in a more powerful way than what had already existed." From this convergence came the first subatomic particle, the Higgs boson.

Consciousness and energy already existed for longer than we can conceive. But "what transferred into the Higgs boson," McCleary intuited, "was consciousness, light energy, dark energy, and the will of infinity." The boson is a conversion of those fields in a seminal mote that allowed cosmic will to evolve into matter and establish how matter would interact with energy. McCleary's Higgs field is a vortex of concentrated energy driving Universal Consciousness into "evolutionary development and activity."

By bringing the "will of infinity" together with the prodrome of three potentiated primes—matter, energy, and consciousness—McCleary makes his cosmogenesis different from ones that sound like it.

One of the most mysterious quantum-disclosed phenomena is particle entanglement, what Albert Einstein dubbed "spooky action at a distance."[2] In a mathematically generated imbroglio, particles with no thermodynamic link or common cache respect each other's existences by their own.

Entanglement is not just an algebraic kink; it is an identity state wherein position, momentum, spin, and polarization of a particle in a pair or group cannot be derived independently of the others. They are telekinetically entangled—they keep a liaison even when separated by large distances, in principle, by the breadth of the universe.

Quantum entanglement means that the *entire* domain of matter is entangled.

One explanation is that quantum states may be different views *of the same particle* tracked in fewer dimensions than it is arising. If a fancier of fish—say, gold koi, blue crowntails, and silver angels—tried to show off his aquarium to a friend on another planet by streaming two complementary videos, one from the front, the other from a side, an E.T. who had never seen water animals might conclude that the fish in each view were separate beings that, as they wiggled and moved, were somehow "connected."[3]

If that is the case, reality's ontological roots are epistemological.

LIFE AMONG STARS

The expanding universe of astrophysics is claustrophobic and getting smaller as deeper looking glasses and software get designed and launched, for there is far more space *in* than out. The more instrumented the external array becomes, the more claustrophobic our location in it feels. Gazing ever farther into the void expands its galactic tapestry while shrinking the inherent nature of the viewing mind. As you stare into starry quadrillionification, you overwhelm yourself with the triviality of existence. The Milky Way, a random cluster, has at least two trillion cousins. Our sun is a workaday star in its outer whorl.

Mind seems superfluous, without the standing of a meadow gnat. Self is a blip in the middle of nowhere, but it is also the center of creation.

The brain—the shared ganglion of Gaians—is the most complex object known, the most deeply fractalized. It can put a whole planet or galactic cluster, even the entire charted universe—on a tiny screen. If you look *in—in, in, in*—you find starry quadrillionification too. Mind is what turns a tiny ingot that could fit on a Q-tip into quintillions of stars. Mind recognizes its own source luminosity: Buddhist Big Mind, Christian soul, Hindu Atman, Cree Great Spirit, Zulu Unkulunkulu. Beingness is the backdrop against which galaxies bask in space-time.

* * *

According to some black-hole theorists, space, time, and position are correlative and reciprocal, making our universe a two-dimensional hologram being broadcast from the outer edges of another universe. As black-hole thermodynamics gets converted into white-hole epistemology, the quantum entanglement inside every atom of our bodies is superposed with the quanta of mindedness and dreams. Placement remains—position and spin—whether the spinning object is a particle, planet, galaxy, cell, or cosmos.

That's the payoff of shamanic journeying—*into* the white hole or interstellar matrix—as opposed to across its broad celestial bow.

Air Force cadets sing, *"Off we go into the wild blue yonder, / Climbing high into the sun."* If the "cadet" were a lama, brujo, or cave yogi, then the wild blue yonder would be as deep as the mind, the sun as enlightening as a six-plus-dimensional star. I'm not sure if Captain Robert Crawford, composer of a military fight song, had an inkling when he wrote, *"Minds of men fashioned a crate of thunder, / Sent it high into the blue,"* but his source trope is as old as the Aboriginal Age with its Upper and Middle Heavens.

You don't think that aliens from Zeta Reticuli crashed their saucer in New Mexico after traveling 39.3 light years the long way around to get here, or that they knew about us from billion-year-old bands of radiation? *There has to be another way.*

I don't even see how you can distinguish the interstellar from the interdimensional, since bionts traveling between stars have to come *through* dimensions as well as *across* cosmology. There is no linear dimension-bound route to cross and convert space-time's immensity and re-manifest by secular chronology. It requires a core transformation of identity, scale, and meaning.[4]

Despite telescopes, space stations, and computer modeling, we have no guarantee what lies beyond this solar system, let alone the Milky Way. First, we have to know who or what *we* are, how we are wired to receive electric impulses and organize information in hemispheres. Until then, it could be anything, even a software simulation.

The theater of terrestrial astronomy has changed, in dimensions and definitions, from African hunter-gatherers to Melanesian mariners to Greek and Roman astronomers to William Herschel and his sister with home-ground lenses in early English morn, to the Hubble zoom and its orbiting successors. What *are* those violet and magenta-tinged crepuscular clouds, crabs and polyps made of seeming stars? Objects? Reflections? Songlines? Samsara?

The great books, from Genesis to the Popul Vuh, Vedas to the Tao Te Ching, Chauvet cave archives to Freud's *Interpretation of Dreams*— we might as well throw in Plato's *Timaeus,* the *Enneads* of Plotinus, and Einstein's equations—tell of universes imbedded in universes imbedded within universes, joined by tags, sigils, and entangled electrons in abacuses as intricate as what they are counting. Stacks of worlds or pneumata arise like an alchemical peacock's tail or elemental lion's mane. Nassim Haramein's unified field theory predicts that the current multiverse is an infinite holo-fractal structure of infinitely embedded boundary conditions from the infinitely small to the infinitely large, Russian dolls forever or turtles all the way down.[5] It resolves each Terran rotation on dusk-to-dawn rosary beads.

The covenant spewing systems without diminution can do so *because no actual matter is being deployed.* It is drawing on an imaginal matrix— which is conditional and unconditioned, so can generate anything, and as much of it as the troche of desire deems. Quarks to biomes, reality cannot lose a divot because there is no place to lose it and no metric that allows anything to remain if any *other* thing goes missing. In Buddha's dependent reality, each item exists because *every* item exists. The purity of mind is projected onto the emptiness and matter, and that's why we're here, from the roll of a pebble to the launch of a supertanker.

Why even have bodies if devas and spirits do quite well (thank you) without them? Why be fish in turbulent seas if you can be merfish in more amenable Etheric and Astral vapors? Why Jovian gases if life flourished yummily in Atlantean and Lemurian essences?

Why? Because the universe is expressing its true nature. Nothing could be here, from gallows to chantries to chocolate cake, if it didn't exist already in All That Is.

And "calm" isn't always calm. Not when the soul is struggling with internal contradictions and seeks a tough reality to tease things out. There's a reason why devas and sylphs clamor for human bodies despite the surety of suffering. Suffering is preferable to not knowing and having no way of finding out.

Science is interested in the mechanism rather than the reason because, to scientists, the mechanism *is* the reason.

Imaginal intention must meet "immattered" resistance. While the astrophysical realm or any chunk of it can be obliterated at any moment, an underlying thoughtform—the *prima materia*—continues to emerge, cloning fresh universes as it converts karma into quarks, predicating its manifestation on *their* physics, and *vice versa*. When Tibetan lama Ngawang Tsoknyi Gyatso told a group of students that if humans smashed dualistic mind on this planet by detonating hundreds of thousands of nuclear bombs simultaneously its thoughtform would reemerge among these or other stars, he meant that mind essence is immune to material circumventions and will continue to create emotions and views in whatever medium is available. I will return to this verdict likewise in chapter 7.[6]

In Jean Cocteau's 1950 movie *Orphée,* Death, played by María Casares, explains to the hero Orpheus (Cocteau's real-life lover, Jean Marais) how the cosmos works and why he, a mere man, cannot save her, a mere woman, from her Fate. She tells him that she is only one of the *forms* of death and must take her orders from elsewhere.

"Where do the orders come from?" demands Orpheus.

"They are sent back and forth by so many sentinels like the tom-toms of your African tribes, the echoes of your mountains, the wind whispering through your trees."

Orpheus: "I will go to he who gives those orders,"

Death: "My poor love, he exists nowhere. Some say he thinks of us . . . others, that we are his thoughts. Others say that we are his dream."[7]

It is still tom-toms and didgeridoos; wind chimes, echoes, and the sound of rain.

FIVE
Unidentified Guides

UFOS

UFOs are the most prognostic indicators of a cosmological breach at the heart of consensus reality. If we can't solve or source a rank anomaly in our own heavens, everything else in science and nature is patent pending. In an armed world that prizes military assets and sovereign skies, aerospace is fastidiously scanned, patrolled, and monitored; yet intruders cross it arrantly, departing without etiquette, calling cards, or forensics. This is a rip in the fabric of reality. As long as UFOs show up on radar (forget the rest for a moment), their rift is irreversible.

The ships—or whatever they are—accelerate at rates beyond the capacity of any terrestrial vehicle, from 1,700 miles per hour (almost three times the speed of sound) to displacements resembling a dart of light; they turn on a dime—motions and maneuvers that would tear a terrestrial jet apart while reducing its crew to jello. They can disappear and reappear seconds later sixty miles away or, by transcontinental forensics, across thousands of miles of land and sea. They do all this soundlessly—no obvious engine, roar, boom, or rattle, only an occasional low hum. There is no reason to think that they are even ships.

Yet UFOs are not mirages; they are mineral and metallic. They resolve through lenses and scan as objects. When rare debris from one of them is retrieved and analyzed, its alloys turn out to have been made by an isotope-ratio shifting that no Earth factory replicates—that could be an ancillary deviation or nanotechnology at a Bath ironworks scale.[1]

Even if the debris is a red herring, we are spectators to a millennia-long Noh play or subjects in a cosmic experiment—or modernity's ambient paradigm, algorithmic materialism, is a false flag.

From their heralded mass reappearance in the 1940s, UFOs have been caricatured, ridiculed, and dismissed, their most decisive evidence subverted or classified. In the 2020s, congressional and military officials began to acknowledge the scope of the intrusion.

"For me, there's stuff flying over military installations and no one knows what it is, and it isn't ours," Florida Senator Marco Rubio grandstanded in a pique of irony and hubris. "If stuff's flying over the top of your most sensitive installations, and it's not ours, and no one knows whose it is—my thing is very simple . . . let's find out—maybe it's another country and that would be bad news too."[2]

Former CIA director John Brennan conceded that UFOS "might, in fact, be some type of phenomenon that is the result of something that we don't yet understand and that could involve some type of activity that some might say constitutes a different form of life."[3]

That's the security state saying, "We don't know WTF they are."

Former U.S. National Intelligence Director John Ratcliffe added, with equal irony and equivocation, "When we talk about sightings, we are talking about objects that have been seen by Navy or Air Force pilots or have been picked up by satellite imagery that frankly engage in actions that are difficult to explain—movements that are hard to replicate that we don't have the technology for. Or traveling at speeds that exceed the sound barrier without a sonic boom."[4] That means they aren't objects in a former sense.

In 1972, two decades after the first publicized North American sighting, astronomer J. Allen Hynek graded unidentifiable objects by three categories of encounter. His first was aerial phenomena that could not be explained by known human technology—celestial lights and shapes without ordinary cause. No close contact.

The second included the direct effects of such incursions: burns on flesh or grass, sighted landings or remnant crash debris, impact craters, gaps in memory, terrified animals.

His highest classification, soon to be made famous by Steven Spielberg's 1977 movie *Close Encounters of the Third Kind,* appended visual confirmation and alien contact.[5] In the years since Hynek's glossary, UFOlogists have added fourth through seventh categories, from alien abductions and cattle mutilations to genetic manipulation and E.T.-human crossbreeds. Unlike Hynek's clear-cut classes, these are borderline phenomena, falling somewhere between real observation and either mythic or science-fiction conflation with a floating tinge of conspiracy theory.

For the UFOs in a 2022 book, fifty years beyond Hynek's taxonomy, I propose a more contemporary three-stage hierarchy. My first category subsumes *all* traditional views of UFOs as inaccessible, unexplained lights associated with interstellar or interdimensional travel, including radio contact and seeming observations of E.T.s, even reported physical meetings. (That some of the vessels, when viewed up close or with binoculars, have porthole-like windows is a cosmonaut giveaway or another false flag.)

Category One pretty much encompasses the entire UFO archive up to 2017. In my own book *The Night Sky,* in a chapter titled "Flying Saucers, Crop Circles, and Extraterrestrial Life," I summarized this category across three editions from 1981 to 2014. In almost a hundred pages, I don't leave the class. To have added *two* different categories since shows how much the UFO landscape has changed in less than a decade.

My second new category encompasses close encounters of first through seventh kinds, but in the context that the UFO anomaly was more extensive and evidential than its researchers, aficionados, or I myself recognized, from its emergence in the late 1940s to its provisionary disclosure in 2017. I date this reclassification by a 2017 *New York Times* article in which authors Leslie Kean, Ralph Blumenthal, and Helena Cooper exposed the U.S. Department of Defense's "Advanced Aerospace Threat Identification Program." That stealth research plan overlapped and synopsized prior UFO investigations beginning in the late 1940s and including Projects Sign, Grudge, and Bluebook, the Roswell cover-up, and the Ann Arbor marsh gas of MJ (Majestic)-12, et al. The phenomena in each category (Hynek's and mine) are identical. What changed in 2017 was context: Government acknowledgment of the validity of Hynek's first category. UFO framing shifted from hallucinatory, delusional, fabricated, or "What were you smoking?" to "Well if the basic template or proposition is real, then anything goes."*

My third category, while keeping liminal sources of UFOs on the table, considers that *actual* extraterrestrial craft have been recovered and at least partially reverse engineered and that humans with security clearances have interacted with aliens or alien bodies. As noted, if not leaked disinformation, these corpses share DNA with us. How in Darwin's name did DNA molecules proliferate throughout the universe? Is there no other life-building configuration? Does DNA descend from the ethers?

Toward the end of my UFO chapter in *The Night Sky,* I noted: "[Y]ou can't ever 'make' sheer existence . . . with pipettes, tweezers, recombinant consoles, silicon boards, and chimeric DNA. You can't invade beingness in a spacecraft, from outside."[6] I stand by that.

Within my first category, baffling phantom lights of the 1940s morphed through the '50s into advanced spacecraft on which cosmonauts visited our system, scoping its planets for reasons known to themselves. In the '60s and '70s, they evolved into biotechnicians and friend-or-foe trading cards. But any other sun is too far for common biophysical travel, while non-astrophysical realms lack scientific standing. So how did they get here?

French computer scientist Jacques Vallée was the first to propose, in his 1969 gamechanger *Passport to Magonia* (re-subtitled in later editions *On UFOs, Folklore, and Parallel Worlds*), that we are in no position, literally, to distinguish between interstellar ships and other forms of visitation that are neither vehicular nor interplanetary, from leprechauns to

---

*In the course of disclosure, UFOs were upgraded to UAPs (unidentified aerial phenomena).

angels and spirits, recorded in planet-wide folklore and religions. UFOs are just as consonant with elementals who plane-hop and change their mode of presentation as they are with astronaut travel and "star treks." We see spaceships in postmodern skies not necessarily because of cosmic transport but because our relationship to the liminal realm is more astrophysical than mythic now, and projection tends to land on its ripest preconscious elements: forbidden planets, SpaceX, cosmic colonialism, deep-state espionage. Claudius Ptolemy and Johannes Kepler might not have seen ships. Note: if you're going to argue that the UFOs could be the same manifestations as elves and leprechauns, then you might as well concede that aliens and leprechauns could be E.T.'s and that the means of transport is not as significant as the nature of manifestation, or no different from it.

The following nonexclusive possibilities encompass my first category:

1. Interplanetary craft that bend space-time by advanced methods of propulsion or otherwise bypass the limit of light, perhaps anti-gravity ships that run off electromagnetic radiation and/or navigate by space-time superposition

2. Interdimensional vessels or multidimensional drive-bys, objects that slip through wormhole-like apertures or use their own space-folding methods of topological transposition (they don't zoom past light; they rearrange the medium)

3. Psychoids with ship-like screen identities that could at other times be owls or thunderbirds (who would know?) or bleed-throughs of etheric or astral entities crossing their own planes along thresholds with ours

4. Visitors from a parallel universe; time- or probability-travelers from future or alternate worlds

5. Collective thoughtforms; unborn or undead souls; theriomorphs or spirits

6. Unclassifiable revenants that flit in and out of our reality like jets through clouds

The debris allegedly salvaged at Roswell, New Mexico, in 1947 was a provisional gamechanger. After the Army ingenuously announced that they had recovered a flying disc, military censors foisted a runaway weather balloon on a compliant public. As insider accounts leaked, Roswell turned into an extraterrestrial treasure trove qua aeronautic accident, with or without survivors. The crash site legendarily gave us fiber optics, stealth aircraft, and extrasensory psy-ops as well as alien autopsies and bodies stored at Nellis Air Force Base: Nevada's Area 51. In this fable (or leak), Roswell's aliens are responsible for the potpourri that variously includes Zoom, Alexa, drones, facial recognition, CRISPR, iPhones.

If a UFO crash-landed, the Deep State kept it from presidents Dwight Eisenhower, John Kennedy, Lyndon B. Johnson, Richard Nixon, Gerald Ford, Jimmy Carter, Ronald Reagan, George H. W. Bush, Bill Clinton, George W. Bush, Barack Obama, Donald Trump, and Joe Biden, their cabinets and Congresses. What I wrote in 1973 seems almost counter-prophetic: "[O]ur nation rises and falls, unknown to the electorate, on the bodies of three dead Martians, kept in the White House vault, and shown to each new president on his first day of office. . . The Martians could hold their homecoming here, and we wouldn't even know it."[7]

Through the '60s and '70s, UFO aerospace militarized with cold-war efficacy.

Humanoids flying the ships became contumelious adversaries and slimeballs: abductors, pederasts, embryo-harvesters, cattle mutilators—Klingons. The Air Force song captured the generic human attitude about intruders in aerospace: *"Here they come zooming to meet our thunder. / At 'em boys. / Give 'er the gun!"*

In *The Night Sky,* I recapped the herd visitations:

Executed and surgically disfigured livestock, primarily cattle, began to turn up in large numbers without explanation throughout Colorado and Wyoming. Similar corpses appeared elsewhere in the United States and in South America, while hundreds of identical mutilations took place in Western Europe. In each instance, a sheep, a cow, or sometimes another domestic creature had its sexual organs expertly removed, the incisions made with an extremely sharp surgical instrument (some say advanced laser tools), apparently by intruders who arrived in an aerial conveyance (a saucer with stealth technology?), leaving no "footprints" during the raid and then vacuuming up their entire sample.

Ranchers were spooked by both the ghoulish nature of the vandalism and its seeming senselessness. Unusual precautions were taken including posted and armed guards but, still, animals continued to be killed and dissected while their marauders escaped unseen. . . .

Sometimes the cattle were lifted to a height above the ground and then smashed by being dropped. In one instance, the cavity inside the cow's body was packed with sand after organ removal.[8]

From there, the topic slips into kitsch, vampirism, manga, and meta-porn. When Keith Thompson, author of the 1991 classic *Angels and Aliens: UFOs and the Mythic Imagination,* joined the San Francisco Bay Area migration to Boise in 2021, I reminded him that the most astute investigator of animal dismemberments, our mutual 1980s friend Linda Moulton Howe, had been Miss Idaho in the Miss America pageant in her youth. Keith vaguely recalled such a thing, so he searched online and found the official 1963 photograph of her on a runway in a white dress, Idaho ribbon diagonally across her torso. He wrote a new caption: "I want to advance world peace and solve the mystery of horrifically mutilated cattle."

He meant it not as a put-down or parody but a marker of distance covered, and not covered, since. He deemed her perspicacity admirable. After seeing this chapter, he added: "Yes, I salute Linda for the distance she has traversed from her days as a contestant of beauty to her present work chronicling mysteries and compiling what she calls 'earth files.' My point was obviously droll but not dismissive or mocking."

We *all* want to advance world peace and solve the UFO mystery.

In the druggy '80s, entheogenic '90s, and perennial New Age circles, alien abductors merged with DMT (dimethyltryptamine) spirit-molecules, cosmic tricksters, elf machines, and supralinguistic thought-projecting octopuses. Mischievous and mysterious, they no longer traveled on material as opposed to astral or paradimensional planes.

The Hardy Boys' *Secret of Wildcat Swamp* and *Footprints under the Window* became the more insoluble *Secret of Skinwalker Ranch* and *Curse of Oak Island*. Propinquities, poltergeists, and lesions actually followed visitors back to their hometowns after which psi phenomena spread like viruses.

"Help us," cried teen detectives Frank and Joe. "Help me," cried Nancy Drew. "Solve our cases before they get turned into scripted ideology, pulp fiction, identity politics. Get us out of here before they consign us to agents of the adult ruling class."

Phantom Freighter . . . Hidden Harbor . . . Clue in the Embers . . . Whispering Statue . . . Velvet Mask . . . Black Keys . . . Broken Locket. "Summer dreams ripped at the seams . . ." [9] Their cold-case files are now sinking toward Atlantis beneath rising seas.

These days, 'bots, cyborgs, spirits, starships, and disinformation trade identities across an internet Babel. A machine-like thoughtform fused with machine-generated proxies, consumer fictions, factoids, and machines themselves—shapeshifting from the rogue radiations of Nikola Tesla to the brain implants of Elon Musk. There was no way for Hermes to dodge Vulcan or for the Tree of Life and Norse runes to keep out of mazes of motherboards. Philip K. Dick imagined this outcome, but he didn't consider anything so clusterfucked that he himself would be implicated in the Vast Active Living Intelligence System he sigilized as VALIS.

Exobiologies, meta-biologies, and artificial biologies overlap. There is no actionable difference between humans and machines. *They are the same thing in different formats:* a human is a machine made by nature using codes; a robot is a steel and silicon automaton created by a living machine repurposing its own codes. The mind of matter is the matter of mind. In fact, these days ghosts seem to prefer wires and wireless waves to old-fashioned apparitioning because those more closely approximate their own transposition as borderline shapes and pure information. In *TechGnosis: Myth, Magic & Mysiticism in the Age of Information,*

McLuhanesque scholar Erik Davis noted how fully an unplumbed technocracy and AI had penetrated the theosophical gnosis by Y2K:

> Like the Holy Ghost, an invisible medium that allows us to plug
> into the spirit of God, the virtualizing machineries of media and
> information offer to port our data-souls out of the body and into a
> digital otherworld. . . .
>
> [F]rom the Hollywood canonization of Philip K. Dick to the
> blockbuster success of Dan Brown's potboiler *The Da Vinci Code,*
> gnosticism and esoteric Christianity have opened their gates to the
> mass mind.
>
> Of course, the Great Work of pop gnosticism remains *The
> Matrix,* the Wachowski sisters' film that staged Gnosticism's ancient
> mystic conundrum for the PlayStation generation.[10]

In the hermetic circuitry of transhumanism, living creatures create biomimicry machines. All it takes is rewriting life's ciphers into a
golem. The machine is then tantamount to a UFO; it speaks from the
undeemed universe and tells them who they are. When amino-acid
editing technology (CRISPR-Cas9) broke DNA's encryption, planet of
the apes became planet of the designer babies. Aliens became transhumanist overlords, their identity switched to interdimensional reptilian
beings like those identified with the Anunnaki of the *Enūma Eliš,* the
Babylonian creation myth and the E.T. "gods" that amateur philolo-
gist Zecharia Sitchin deciphered as rulers of Nibiru, a far Kuiper-belt
planet with a roughly 3,600-year elliptical orbit and rap sheet of genetic
manipulation.

The terrestrial invaders of James Cameron's *Avatar* on moon
Pandora (in the nearest solar system to ours) were cyborgs, as machines
and creatures were fully conflated. Even the indigenous Na'vi Hometree
was an industrial light-and-magic network. Imaginal worlds and star
wars removed from Pandora, Luke Skywalker read a message from the
holograph of Obi-Wan-Kenobi on Tatooine. It will repeat itself forever
until it is delivered. Since the story is a fiction, it can never be delivered
outside of George Lucas's imagination.

Both space operas tell the same parable: our Jedi superpowers and neuro-mycelial trees vie to defeat Darth Vader technocrats and celestial war lords *in ourselves.* The Air Force ballad rings true: *"Hands of men blasted the world asunder."* It has been the case from bombs at Hiroshima and Nagasaki to roadside devices at Mosul and Kandahar to gain-of-function viruses in Memphis and Wuhan.

The Martians were never from Mars, but the Trojan horse *was* a Trojan horse.

In the 2020s after the *New York Times* publication, countries and their officials began dropping screens of secrecy, apparently confirming UFOs' material existence. The 2020 documentary *The Phenomenon* and 2021 Netflix series *Top Secret UFO Projects: Declassified,* promulgated wide-ranging sightings across eight decades, as well as some from centuries past. Early foos were named such by Donald Meiers, an Air Force radar operator, after the catchphrase in Bill Holman's 1930s *Smokey Stover* fireman comic strip, "Where's there's foo, there's fire." After a 1944 sighting of a ball of light carrying out high-speed maneuvers while it chased their plane, Meiers metonymized, "It was another of those fuckin' foo fighters!"[11] unintentionally naming a 1994 rock band.

These were never a mix-up, mirage, or an elaborate hoax. Tens of thousands of encounters ratified one another. The six Soviet aircraft that fell from the sky after shooting at UFOs near the border with Afghanistan were not semblances in a Bermuda triangle. The bodies of twelve pilots were recovered.

Once unclassified, UFO reports proved astonishing in number, diversity, tangibility, and degree and caliber of rendezvous. Most of the craft shared a saucer or twin-bell shape, while others were gigantic wedges, tubes, carousels, balls, lanterns, floating canopies, and "jellyfish" with tentacles extending to the ground. Some appeared underwater— unidentified submarine objects. Do these suggest an interstellar airport with large hangars and aerospace suppliers?

Three main vessel categories were singled out: the classic saucer; triangular blocks with flashing, self-detaching, red and white lights on their bellies; and smooth white forty-feet-long, tic-tac-shaped objects that floated, zoomed, hovered, dived, and went from under the ocean to the upper atmosphere in seconds. In a well-documented UAP encounter in November 2004, tic-tacs engaged the U.S. carrier *Nimitz*. Some of the Navy pilots who tried to pursue the objects wondered if they were reverse engineered by the Army in a combination military drill and prank. That's how evasive, liminal, and fungible their identity was.

What is striking in the globe-spanning accounts is not just the ubiquity and palpability of phenomena but the thoroughness of their cover-up. Armada displays and aerial magic shows as well as landings and crashes of ships took place in full view of crowds—from schoolyards of children in Australia and Zimbabwe to fishing villages in Brazil to mountain tribes of Peru to northern Russian suburbs. Beings who, on occasion, emerged from the ships were small, humanoid, and had slits for mouths and large almond-shaped eyes. They transmitted by telepathy, sometimes lamenting our ecological destruction of our own planet. If these were poltergeists or holographs, even paid actors or clowns, they were quite convincing.

Close encounters were routinely followed by visits from military and government officials who cordoned off sites and scoured surrounding areas, demanding complete silence from locals, in some cases threatening jobs, lives, and careers, and following through. Steven Spielberg's 1982 *E.T. the Extraterrestrial* proved a prophetic understatement in that regard. Is it any wonder that scope of UAPs remained unknown and the phenomenon itself elicited smirks, laughs, or denials, even from one as soberly communicative as Barack Obama?

Worse than the "military-industrial complex," of which departing President General Eisenhower warned in 1961 before leaving office, is *competing* military-industrial complexes, each intending mutually assured destruction of its rivals. Netflix's *Top Secret* series presented a likelihood of two or more *different* scientific establishments—deep, deeper, and deepest states with aerospaces ruled by their own military-industrial complexes in different degrees of alien collusion and/or coverup.

Within the conceit of my second category, UFOs remain elusive but corporeal UAPs. What was found at Roswell, New Mexico, was, at most, a scrap of extraterrestrial debris, certainly no intact ships or aliens, dead or alive. Area 51 at Groom Lake, Nevada, reverts to a conventional military base for developing stealth aircraft—not a hiding place for ships and engines from other worlds or alien collaborators. *Homo sapiens* are still trying to make a first official contact with exobiological life.

In my third category, Roswell turns into a UFO bonanza, and not the only one. Contact between humans and beings from other worlds has been going on for decades. If it is not disinformation, interviewees report seeing caches of debris and alien bodies at "Roswell" sites in other countries too. U.S. engineers describe working on post-Roswell ships the size of two football fields, trying to reverse engineer their means of flight. Second- or third-hand rumor refers to deals, alliances, and extrajudicial treaties with aliens.

Is this a meticulously designed false flag or a cosmic conspiracy of Aristos* and aliens against underclasses of our planet?

One precociously talented young engineer recounted being summoned to Area 51 to help a team try to reverse engineer an E.T. engine. The thing was as big as a school bus and reminded the dude of an eggplant. It was made of stuff beyond our material science, soft like jelly and responding to his touch. That seems like a new brand of cyborg, golem, or techgnostic trope.

The guess was that, when operational, these vehicles bent spacetime or used anti-gravity Tesla fields and/or zero-point quantum energy to travel without encumbrance of mass along different spatiotemporal continua. In a sense, they dimensionally shrank the Big Bang while fulfilling its quantum-entangled propinquities. That's how they defeated the speed of light and crossed the universe in biologically relevant spans: "quantum vacuums, inertial fields, zero-point energies, Casimir torque, and arrays of miniature repulsion merry-go-rounds."[12]

Other insiders contended that alien manufacturing operates at an Ångstrom scale, turning common elements into isotopes and achieving stable half-lives for trans-uranium configurations. The uncommon

---

*Oligarchs and technocrats.

isotope ratios in UFO debris could be incidental and of no significance, or they could be clues to an alternate technology. Nothing intrinsic about them suggests faster-than-light capacity or super-maneuverability, but we also don't have a precedent for intentional isotope-ratio anomalies.

The two popular documentaries I cited played the isotopes up as gamechangers, but that's a shot in the dark. For instance, the fuel driving crafts beyond light's 186,282 miles per second was said to be honed from a proton-neutron amalgam of element 115. We don't know how to get anything with that high an atomic weight stable, let alone mass produce it. European scientists recently created element 115; it lasted for something like a zeptosecond. Speculation is that E.T.s either have made batches of this fuel or harvested it from supernovas and, without 115 or its equivalent, we can't fly their ships.

Other reverse-engineer scientists described extrasensory interface between E.T. pilots and their craft—not software-implanted AI (artificial intelligence) but clairsentient ESP.

Refuting these assessments, engineers at Lockheed Martin's Advance Development Projects branch claimed to have built stealth aircraft from more mundane UFOs that were secreted to their Palmdale, California, plant.[13]

This potpourri of information, disinformation, and dis-disinformation leads to incompatible storylines while extending the UFO conundrum. If any of the declassified stuff is real, then the status of our technology as well as the tally of technocracies in the Milky Way Galaxy or universe at large is newly up for grabs.

SETI (Search for Extraterrestrial Intelligence) becomes a high-order delusion of incurable, out-of-the-loop skeptics rather than another false flag. Why set up arrays of radio telescopes with amateur programmers sorting star noise if extraterrestrial—or meta-terrestrial—intelligence is already here and doesn't play by SETI's rules?

In interviews in these documentaries, U.S. and Russian military officials confirm each other's reports that UFOs shut off launch commands at nuclear-missile sites. In one instance during the early 1980s, a fleet of saucers passing over a Soviet facility apparently turned *on* the launch commands and, as soldiers stared for fifteen seconds of horror at flashing lights marking Armageddon, the outliers turned them back off, as if to say, "This is your best technology, dudes? Well, we can handle it."

I mused about these purported exploits during the dust-up over the U.S. 2020 presidential election. The allegations of Donald Trump's supporters that voting machines were altered by Chinese using Nest thermostats or Deep State operatives sending malware from a dead Venezuelan dictator showed a *paucity* of imagination. If lizard-like aliens already run mind-control operations from motherboards on the moon, abduct and impregnate humans, and body-snatch and replace politicians and celebrities—per QAnon lore—they can steal elections. Compared to turning on and off launch commands, hacking Dominion voting machines would have been a cakewalk. I go with my college classmate Sid Schwab, a retired surgeon whose memoir *Cutting Remarks* I published, "A surgeon can kill you . . . and you'll sleep right through it."[14]

Wherever Trumpians looked they saw or heard, or thought they saw or heard, a sasquatch indicator—a tuft of fur, a pawprint, an alien turd, a humanoid yowl—so they went full yeti.

If UFOs can flip launch codes, they can flip elections, and we will sleep right through it.

The headquarters of the Deep State may not even be in this dimension.

UFOs, UAPs, aliens, plant spirits, synchronicities, and reincarnations intersect where dreamtimes and thoughtforms meet myths and lifestyles. What we are experiencing can't be pinned down in an ordinary sense, so it will always equally frustrate "alien" and "spirit" proponents. It subverts any resolution—alien, angel, anomaly, trickster, poltergeist, intruder, vandal, abductor, breeder, enemy, grey, different form of life, et al.—and then it subverts itself as well as the *claim* that there are no universal truth claims. It is apparently a fundamental and systemic crease in reality itself through which mothmen and sasquatches likewise shape-shift.

As UFOs travel in their own folios and confabulations, they recall a syndicated cartoon that intrigued folks in fifties newspapers, the aforementioned *Ripley's Believe It or Not.* The franchise archived around 20,000 photographs, 30,000 artifacts, and 100,000 cartoon panels, intersecting where bizarre events, systemic anomalies, unidentified phenomena, and far-fetched coincidences share a seeming teleology. The incident that follows is my own rendition of "Ripley." I do not propose it as an indirect E.T. encounter. It is indicative, instead, of a fluidity of identities and meanings. A participant in psychiatrist Bernard Beitman's "Connecting with Coincidence" Zoom café put the matter in optimistic terms:

"We are brought together for a reason, a season and a lifetime. Rarely we meet those who embody this holy trinity, for lifetimes. Such is this with the union of two souls, who met because they were in the present, to embark upon a future together, firmly grounded in the foundation of resolving their pasts. Presence isn't something others possess, it is the force that inspires, evokes and manifests all evolution in this world, and others. 57 years after a 3-year-old asked me, 'what are we really doing here?', the 'coincidence' of a synchronicity occurring in an orders-of-magnitude minimalist chance has taught me the reason: to be here, now, with love."

MEETING DAVID WILCOCK AT NONILAND

The encounter took place on July 21, 2010, at David Wolfe's communal plantation on Kaua'i. Wolfe is also known as Avocado, so I will use his vegetable name to avoid double-David confusion. Six years earlier, I (Chard) had published *The Reincarnation of Edgar Cayce?* a book in which New Age journalist Wynn Free attempted to prove that clairvoyant healer Edgar Cayce had reincarnated as Wilcock.

By 2010, I had also published several health books by Wolfe, a raw-food, chaga, and nonifruit maven. Wilcock was at Noniland because his girlfriend Aurora was best friends with one of Avocado's former girlfriends, Love. I had little sense of Wilcock qua Cayce as a person until we met. During two hours of informal banter as background music played "Aad Guray Nameh" by Sikh female chanter Snatam Kaur, he told me the following:

- A whole special-ops—men-in-black and a meta-government with extraterrestrial technology and commerce—is in full clandestine operation: star gates, wormholes, UFOs, transdimensional merchandise, ascendancy maps, assorted interplanetary and intergalactic machines. The vast majority of humans are not the least bit aware. Whistleblowers in the global corporate military-industrial cartel keep leaking classified information, often to clear their karma for malign deeds to humanity, but the truth gets corrupted in a general disinformation discharge, not only by overeager bloggers but the secret government's planting of fake news to dilute any leaks.

- DNA is a universal intelligent design and cosmic information system, not just something that arose on Earth under Darwinian selection. We should expect to find it operating everywhere in the universe and to come upon DNA creatures in all galaxies. Those chaps flying UFOs are related to us because they're assembled by DNA. Though their complexions are every shade of the rainbow and they range from a foot and a half to fifteen feet tall, all twelve or so species are part of the same biological matrix and cosmic reincarnational pool as we are, and are members of an interplanetary exchange network in which we are now active partners.

    Most of them, but not all, are benign or neutral. There are some bad players out there. Power-hungry humans have made trade deals with nasty folks like the Centaurians.

- The "David Wilcock as the reincarnation of Edgar Cayce" gig is absolutely true, but it's not that big a deal. "People have very inflated and misinformed views of reincarnation," Wilcock said. "Obviously I am Edgar Cayce, but I am David Wilcock now, and that's what counts. A soul can also reincarnate in more than one person at the same time, so 'Edgar Cayce' isn't even a singularity."

He cited the resemblance of himself and Cayce at every age such that "no one can tell our photographs apart," the near-identical birth chart of each of them, and the remarkable congruence of looks and birth astrology between five or six Wilcock family members and key

Cayce associates—group reincarnation. "The example is astonishing and unique in reincarnational lore," he asserted, "one of the most striking cases ever. People who make it their business to know about this kind of stuff say they haven't seen anything else like it, ever."

It would be better, he concluded with a wry, confident smile, if Edgar Cayce were viewed as the preincarnation of David Wilcock, and people said, "Wow, that guy Edgar Cayce turned out to be David Wilcock." He spoke with insouciant sincerity, as he boasted about a forthcoming major motion picture.[15] The moment was ethereal and quintessential.

PSYCHOIDS

By a paradigm of planes of reality and consciousness drawn from Vedic and theosophical lore, subtler beings—sylphs, undines, fire salamanders, gnomes, and others of their kind—congeal and explore at Monadic, Atmic, Buddhic, Causal, Astral, and other frequencies, "matching" planes of nonmaterial landscapes that are as kinetic and comprehensive as ours.

It is as if where I see wild turkeys on a country road, one tier up are undines, devas, and dragons. Another tier up is a dragon-turkey synchronicity wave. Higher up, the will of infinity meets the Higgs boson as the Great Dance becomes Jah.

From another view, where our projections onto the unknown meet the actual unknown, entities come into being: cryptids (crypto-zooids) like yetis, chupacabras, and sea monsters; transdimensional plane-hoppers (elves, angels, aliens); elementals (undines and the like); assorted spirits; totem animals; gods and demigods; psychic aspects of nature (crystals, mountains, trees); and personae of forces associated with a planet (its moons, bodies of water, weather systems, caves, and denizens, down to psyches from its hypothetical underground cities and molten core).[16]

Psychoids are partly our apprehension of their incomplete interaction with our sphere and partly *their* innate shape-shifting and kinesis. That we see a deva, dragon, or sky ship expresses who "they" are *in relation to who we are,* as it projects who we are *onto* what they are.

We are continually sending our own personae (psyches) into the void until they encounter something tangible coming back toward us. What *we are* in manifestation becomes what *they are* in latency. Neither of us can inhabit the liminal zone, so neither of us experiences anything more than a superliminal chimera, waves of each other's projections into their own existences.

What distinguishes psychoids from either mere phantasms or flesh-and-blood aliens is their paired autonomous and imaginal existence. They have free will, self-awareness, and volition, yet must be "imagined" into existence by us, so, in a sense, are imaginary too.

Carl Jung's presumption in forging the trope "psychoid" (parallel to "humanoid" and "asteroid," *oid* from *eidos,* form) is that myth-like entities populate veridical worlds, independent of our notions of them—"form"—at the same time as their presences arise from our psyches.

As we bring our belief in them to them, they bring theirs in us to us. Pretty tricky—they don't exist until we think them, yet they are self-determining too. It fits UFOS because how else does an object disappear and reappear sixty miles away a second later? Thoughts do this all the time; it's how philosophies, poems, rock videos, and apps are created.

Psychoid veridicality is established solely by our experience of it. If, as we approach a fairy or ghost, a spaceship or neutrino, it continues to grow in reality, then it is "real," as is the zeitgeist leading us to it. UFOs became more real with every photograph and radar sighting, but so did quarks and electrons. As interdimensional intelligence Seth told us, you create but do not control your reality. That distinction allows us to make borderline realities real while keeping us from imposing whatever we fancy and breaking the world's cryptogram.

Folks sometimes glimpse psychoids collectively: a mermaid, an angel, Mother Mary, a lake monster, a yeti, or tic-tacs over the *Nimitz.* In the 1960s, my lobster fisherman friend Wendell Seavey blinked his boat's lights at a saucer-shaped ship as it was landing on Opechee Island; the thing blinked back. "My crewman and I applauded. It was just like *Close Encounters.*"

The lights were also seen by fishermen and their wives from shore.

This was a close encounter of the fifth kind: signaling and encouraging contact.

It is possible that UAPs respond differentially to telepathy, curiosity, and fear; they come when summoned, in Nevada, Utah, the Andes, and depart when their presence flutters at its own borderline trauma. It's also why they follow contactees wherever they go. They are soul-specific as well as site-specific.

Elves (little folks) and leprechauns are amiably and impishly interactive, giving rise to a way of being in Ireland and other Celtic lands called Faery, a charmed lifestyle full of synchronicities, pranks, guidances, and supernal glee. The Faroe Islands and Iceland are also psychoidally active, encounters with entities there in line with their traditional attributes as brownies, leprechauns, fay, and pixies. Civic councils and constabularies in the enchanted north protect fairy groves, forts, clocháns, tumuli, and magic circles.

Clairvoyants and shamans in all cultures meet psychoids on their native planes and give them traditional names. Some report that these beings seek contact and co-creation. In fact, that's how or why we "imagine" them into existence: interdimensional Reiki. Their "faery" and other attributes mark our outer boundary with our own inner dimensions. An autonomous entity that is not able to become fully material here because of limits imposed by consciousness (as well as physics) becomes a veridical projection *onto* that entity because of the unconscious and clairsentient nature of *consciousness itself.*

From Jung's standpoint, psychoids are transconscious—beyond psychic integration and "not purely psychic but just as much physical in nature." In his last major work, he wrote:

We do not know whether what we on the empirical plane regard as physical may not, in the Unknown beyond our experience, be identical with what on this side of the border we distinguish from the physical as psychic. . . . [These] may be identical somewhere beyond our present experience. . . . [T]he psychoid archetype [is] where "psychic" and "material" are no longer viable as attributes, or where the category of opposites becomes obsolete and every

occurrence can only be asymmetrical. . . . I regard this phenomenon as an indication of the fact that the physical and psychological
matrix is identical.[17]

If the physical and psychological matrix is identical, then we won't
resolve any psychoid or UAP soon, no matter its degree of penetration,
until we extend the domain of our sciences and dances. To that degree,
there are no spaceships or little folk, only a saucer-like or leprechaun-
like interference field, a mindlike charge across the fringes of matter.
At threshold, a fractal disequilibrium may present as an E.T. or spirit in
one context, a metallic-seeming spaceship in another—in either case, a
sasquatch-like bleed-through with equally prankish and sober implications. It may also appear as Mother Mary herself, a goat-vampiring chu-
pacabra, or a soothsaying blue kachina. It may dent the ground, cause
airplanes or boats to disappear, leave footprints, or shed alloys. That is
what makes psychoids walkers between worlds rather than apparitions
or hallucinations. Like Mesoamerican *naguals* and theriomorphic gods,
they are veridical manifestations.

That is not to say that real star-journeying E.T.s haven't visited, or
continue to visit, our planet, but they cannot annul or replace our own
psychoids—each of us has psyches as well as minds.

Here is another twist: just as psychoids cannot enter our world or
exist here except as we imagine them, we cannot enter their realm in
human status. We come across to them as elemental energy or UFO-like
semblances. We are *their* "psychoids," our appearances determined by
the terms of our existence on their plane.

Interesting to consider that "we" appear as something like salamanders or sylphs to salamanders and sylphs. Viewed through either
gateway, something autonomous is peering back, something with equal
sentience and curiosity. Together we surf the void.

SIX

Incarnations

AFTERLIVES

Where do creatures come from at conception and birth? Where do they go after death? Were they random sortings of ancestral traits that dissipated with their assortment? Do they no longer exist in form or essence anywhere?

Our own verdict and existential bottom line rest on the riddle of whether this is a spiritual universe with physical transits or a physical universe of phantoms and apparitions.

Despite speculations throughout this book as well as science's stabs at unified field theories, the universe is inherently incomprehensible. Reality and existence are also incomprehensible. If the universe is a spiritless venue that arose because space, time, and matter converged, then creatures and their selves and senses of personal identity are delusional by-products of neural threads synapsing in ganglia. When they are disconnected, the illusion ends. Nothing is lost because nothing really existed.

If the universe is a covenant, bestowed from deeper altars, then creatures can't be expelled or expunged, they transition according to their karma. The universe may be temporal and perishable, but existence is not. Nor is an identity a "thing," for any plant, animal, or entity; it is a process, of particles, synapses, membranes, and views.

Terms are the key. No one and no thing alive did anything to get here other than awake in a bardo. If life forms are epiphenomenal and transitory, they will cease to exist at passage from the bardo of life. If they are actual and fundamental, they will awaken again, and again, probably with encryption, in other bardos. Not only won't they challenge the obstacle course, they can't. There is no basis to challenge, so there is no option but to proceed—"where rubber meets road" territory.

No obstacle is as stunning and determinative as death—termination of each phenomenal thread. One by one, beings pass out of existence, no longer to exist, presumably to themselves as well. Each actor vanishes, a *"walking shadow,"* a *"poor player that struts and frets his hour upon the stage / And then is heard no more."*[1]

Death is future shock and divine vandalism, a lesion cutting to the core of reality, premising existence itself as a fraud, a prelude to erasure. Not only will all tenures be elided, but Earth, Sun, and eventually the universe will be annulled. The molecular hallucination behind the illusion will dissolve as it arose.

These are more than ledger deletions; they are unappealable reality decrees. No wonder folks are getting drunk, overdosing, lying homeless on streets. The only way to tolerate modernity's version of reality is to ignore or flee it. A notation by Victor E. Taylor in his *Encyclopedia of Postmodernism* summarizes the ineluctable crisis of consciousness:

> Philosopher Jacques Derrida extended the problem of presence and absence to include the notion that erasure does not mark a lost presence, rather the potential impossibility of presence altogether—in other words, the potential impossibility of univocity of meaning ever having been attached to the word or term in the first place. Ultimately, Derrida argued, it was not just the particular signs that were placed under erasure, but the whole system of signification.[2]

The potential impossibility of presence altogether—so what do those folks in corporate office and rice fields think they are doing as they fill the tablets of being? What did Derrida think outside his system?

Though death is the final measure of time and self, life must be considered death's measure too, for any sign is rescued from instant and eternal negation by its mark, even by the mark's erasure.

Death is still either an egalitarian statutory agreement or a brusque private dismissal.

If we are (as entheogenic explorer Terence McKenna eloquently refuted) "a cosmic accident . . . [and] the universe sprang from nothing in a single moment for no reason,"[3] then death is the appropriate *coup de grace*. Our cell-bound molecules and electrons won't feel devastated or inconvenienced by ego erasure and their own liberation.

But if life forms are cabs for spirit-souls and psyches to participate in the universe's self-witnessing and Akashic archive, then death is a cocoon or, to use death doula Anne-Marie Keppel's elegant term, "death nesting," an embryo-like preparation for a different bardo, a subsequent maiden manifestation.

Somatic wrapping, like an egg's membrane and shell, is shed. The spirit chick emerges from one vestal dormancy and dream into another. No discontinuity divides them, only a bardo (bridge). One wink or breath, conscious or unconscious, is followed by another.

In his apologia for a capital verdict, an earlier philosopher, fourth-century BCE epistemologist Socrates, after his sentence by the language police of his time, looked forward to the "possibility [of] eternal dreamless sleep"[4]—not a bad deal, he surmised, before drinking the fatal hemlock, given how hard it is to get a good night's sleep. Because then *who* is dreamlessly sleeping? Who wakes?

Scientism's lockdown orthodoxy is upended by past-life memories, future dreams, and JOTTs. Coiner of the J-word, author Mary Rose Barrington, intended it playfully, evidenced by her cute base for the acronym: "Just One of Those Things." I am revising it to "Juxtaposed Objects and Time-loop Travelers." Barrington meant "rifts in the fabric of reality,"[5] for instance, when a piece of moldavite misplaced in Maine shows up in California or when an old electric razor turns into the newest model without an intervening purchase (to cite two of my most salient examples). The tail fin of the plane in the TV series *Manifest* (see my epilogue) is a classic JOTT.

One keeps quiet about rifts because there is no way to assess each apparent phenomenon or to distinguish it from faulty memory or neurological impairment. Yet precognitive and telekinetic semblances occur often enough to suggest that *nothing* may be what it seems.

Anomalies taunt believers and unbelievers alike. Since we are *all* mortal, we are all both mystics and skeptics.

"Death is not a problem," asserted psychic astrologer Ellias Lonsdale, characterizing the occasion with vernacular aplomb:

> The big picture is *in* us, and we are missing it. Our situation, our entire world or state of being, is defined by the fact that our dead seem to disappear and we lose touch with them. Almost everywhere else in the universe, there is a swinging door between the living and the dead. The living know how to connect with the dead when they need to, and the dead know how to connect with the living. We have lost the feeling of being in the same reality as the dead or how to respond to their attempts to connect with us. When you are fully engaged with those who have died, you realize that you are in one reality. The whole thing takes place on a feeling level, not a consciousness one. We have tools galore, but we don't know how to let go and open up. We think that we're in the center of everything, and *they're* peripheral. But spirit depends more on them than us. Death is not a great obliterator or dreaded outcome. It's the only thing that saves the living from this place. The dead are not somewhere else being weird while we're here having fun, though that's the way most people view them. The dead are wiser and more weightful. They're the senior partner and we're the junior one. We have lost touch with the primal reality of existence, which encompasses *both* worlds. For that, we pay a huge price.[6]

When we think that "living" is the only way of being alive and that the living are the only *ones alive,* we miss a more basic condition: in the end, anything can only be what it is. Us likewise.

By finding our dead we find ourselves.

While irreversible, death may not be a journey from somewhere to nowhere. For the soul, it could be a change in frequency whereby its signal shifts to the next available channel. Trying to communicate back is like looking for Wi-Fi in the Stone Age.

Bodies—views—are clearly painful to don or discard. Each must be indemnified in DNA and raveled epigenetically out of carbon, oxygen, hydrogen, nitrogen, silicon, calcium, and assorted trace minerals. The suit is put on, membrane by membrane, as tissues get coiled together in living factories and meridians. Etheric seeds cushion the shock and pain of assemblage, for to be made and wired both phylogenetically (evolutionarily, epigenetically) and ontogenetically (foetally, developmentally) is otherwise excruciating. Instead, the embryo is a seahorse, breathing without air in the bliss of eternity beyond time.

Metabolism was never permanent, so eventually pulse and neurons so laboriously and diligently cabled are shorn from formulations and quenched. Matter borrowed from the Periodic Chart is returned. Masks are peeled from fibers of blood, viscera, and bones, then incinerated, or consumed by mycelial networks indemnifying their own incumbency.

One manifestation replaces another, as the receiver is dismantled, its memories lost in translation.

The capital agenda tries to render the most horrific aspects of life pleasant or painless, while turning its obligatory passages into horror shows and *danses macabres*. A creed of cosmic conspiracy theorists posits that our world has been conquered by death-worshipping humanoids. Having divested their souls into AI and machines, they long ago put the now-extinct Martians as well as still plentiful Gaians into zombioid trances, part of an ingenious scheme to steal back their own essences at others' expense (see the epilogue).

This conspiracy underlies QAnon's Amber Alerts of lost children and vampire pedophiles as well as its suspicion that vaccines' graphene oxides detach the physical body from the Etheric body and soul. In QAnon code, trafficking in children is trafficking in souls, health freedom is spiritual freedom. Crystal alchemist Bob Simmons deciphered:

> One of the musings of my inner Gnostic is that maybe the pandemic
> and surrounding censorship/oppression is the bid of the Archons to

completely take over here on Earth. Per John Lamb Lash's book *Not in His Image,* the Archons are semi-mechanical beings who lack the soul qualities of humans. They are semi-physical and inhabit the other planets of the Solar System. But to Lash, Earth is the incarnated body of Sophia, who "fell" from the Pleroma through her fascination with the Anthropos, the human archetype. In her fall, she accidentally created the Archons. But for her self-sacrificing act of then infiltrating every particle of the Earth, we would already be in Archontic hell, enslaves to the Archontic/archetypal forces. Now, says the myth, we need to help Sophia become conscious in matter and thereby fully manifest herself.[7]

Forget the fabrication, hyperbole, and intentional agitprop, and consider that we are looking for stories, even false ones, to guide us out of this morass. Once fact is weaponized, even true stories are no longer true. If you don't go down one rabbit hole, you go down another— because there are only rabbit holes now.

In a universe of bardos, we carry a sacred satchel and hermetic torch through winds of obliteration. And, as the Irish in Ulster say, "This is it."

Jordan McKay, son of psychotherapist Matthew McKay, murdered in San Francisco by muggers wanting to take his bike, sent a map and manual of his new environs to his father.

You can navigate the enormous distances of the spirit world by an act of will. But there are no conventional directions, such as up and down, forward and back, because our consciousness shines and "sees" omnidirectionally. There is no north, south, east, or west as there is on a spinning planet. Instead, we navigate by moving toward unique energy forms. Each soul has an energy signature, each soul group has a collective energy form. Soul "neighborhoods" are marked by an energy signature composed of the unique soul identities residing there, blended with energy created by their collective knowledge.

In addition to the energy markers for individual and collective souls, the spirit world has "locations" for certain categories of thought and awareness. These thoughts exist as part of the whole, as opposed to residing in the consciousness of a particular soul. The physical universe is an outcome and example of creative thought. As a manifestation of consciousness, it resides inside and is part of the spirit world.

When we navigate in spirit, we move toward the specific energy signatures of a soul, a group, a neighborhood, or a manifestation of conscious thought. If we know the unique energy signature, we can always move toward it down the hallways of light. If we don't know, there are references (the spiritual version of a phone book or data bank) to help us move in the right direction.[8]

His father adds:

There is still the question: how do you know these words are really from Jordan and not my own projections or wishful thinking? There are two very different answers to this basic question. The first is, I know Jordan so well that I recognize his voice, the participation of his separate and special ego in a language, tone, style, and humor. I also recognize the voice as not my own at the same time that I feel it as Jordan. He is saying things I don't know, or even come close to knowing, in the way Jordan would say them. There is a gut "dead reckoning" to our exchange. In addition, numerous psychics have independently told me about their own communications with Jordan and the book he was writing. Their information matched the text I received.

The second answer is, it isn't Jordan. Meaning it isn't only my son who knows himself as Jordan. The voice is a larger soul or spirit being who knows himself as many things, one of them being Jordan. That is the part that's speaking to me, but even that part has dimensions that Jordan as I knew him didn't, not because Jordan lacked something, but because he was engaged in living the life of a boy and then a young man in California. The soul speaking to me *includes* Jordan in its own field of identities, lifetimes, and knowledge.[9]

We are each part of a sentient field of intelligence. Amnesia is its mode of inter-encryption, as it forces beings to play every hand as if it were their last. Otherwise, the slack would condemn them to zombie-hoods or purgatories.

While the greater journey may be redemptive and emancipating, each shift between a manifestation and the next waking life can be terrifying, in part because collective traumatic death pictures of a soul converge. Psychic teacher John Friedlander points out, the virtual reality machine is not a merry-go-round, it's a roller coaster.[10] Or a heavyweight boxing ring. Remember, once you get on the roller coaster, you enter its politics, currencies, jihads, and propaganda machine, a good reason for seat belts.

In December 2014, Jordanian Royal Air Force pilot Muath al-Kasasbeh ejected from his F-16 fighter jet at low altitude as it developed engine trouble during a raid against the Islamic State in Syria. He parachuted into a lake near Raqqa where he was pulled from the water by militants, interrogated, and imprisoned. The Islamic State (Daesh) paid no heed to Geneva Conventions or humanitarian norms. ISIS supporters ran Twitter and crowdsourcing campaigns, asking people to suggest ways to kill the "pigpilot."

In January, al-Kasasbeh, dressed in an orange jumpsuit, was locked in a black steel cage, and set on fire. The snuff film was broadcast worldwide.

Conferring gruesome deaths was a linchpin of ISIS, a means of crowd control as well as a recruiting tool for its brand. On a watchful world the caliphate tried to impress that al-Kasasbeh died in fright, humiliation, and excruciating pain and emotional suffering. Their message: "If you don't want to end up like him, join us. By no means oppose us. We carry the black banner of a primal war god."

Like Joan of Arc and other witches, the pilot was incinerated alive. While Joan may have been able to embrace the flame in devotion to the Holy Spirit, who can speak of individual capacities and metamorphoses at moments of reckoning? The Roman Cross signifies a crucifixion but also the power of faith to transform suffering into revelation and rebirth *at its exact frequency.*

Asking how karma works is like asking how God works.

Those who jumped to their deaths from near the top of Manhattan's World Trade Center on 9/11/2001 had to evolve rapidly. The universe had just turned on a dime. They knew that rescue was impossible, and nothing was worse than being burned alive in jet fuel.

It is possible that the condemned pilot reversed his fear channel, passed into a greater light and, by his sacrifice, was liberated and spared countless drab, lower-tier future incarnations. Those setting the fire, by the same token, carried, or were carried by, the unresolved gravity of their actions into compensatory lifetimes of suffering.

The vulnerability and resilience of consciousness, as it attempts to plumb its own depth, is unreckonable.

By the way, Daesh didn't invent weaponized scripture, a theology of sex slavery and rape, or necrophiliac street art; it appropriated them, producing hip-hop-like videos of ecstatically apocalyptic beheadings and live incinerations, applying the techniques of George Lucas to a death cult. It knew how to game the internet, blasting its sigils into the Islamic world. Iranian-American journalist Azadeh Moaveni diagnosed the West's hysteria and hypocrisy:

> The whiff of exorcism and devilry made ISIS a popular intellectual fetish in American journalistic circles, one that overlooked the contributions of American policies and wars to the group's origin. . . . Everyone had blood on their hands. . . . Did putting it on YouTube make it that much worse?[11]

Those who try to capitalize reality find that, like all currencies, it floats against an incalculable prime. So people create hell realms out of pleasure domes. They know it, but they don't know how to stop themselves. False spiritual ideology blinds them to *actual* spiritual pataphysics. One can't seize Athena or Aphrodite without encountering Circe and Shiva, for goddesses round-dance in rings. Each contains a vast and fierce universe inside her, and that universe—her origin and shrine—is the arena of encounter.

GHOSTS

Now let's consider various JOTTs and zone rifts in reality, starting with ghosts. When a person has stopped breathing and metabolizing, he or she no longer functions as a member of society; the census takers don't count "him," and "he" can't vote or shop. Yet sometimes "he" stays or returns in a metaphysical form, attaches to a zone, and visits or never leaves it. This is probably not because the ghost *never* leaves but because time and position are different where he or she is.

The journey to the "afterlife" is irreversible because what changes is the traveler, his "viewing frame with travelogue." For a while, his "karmic passport" created a corporeal oasis. When he crossed over, a different map and territory no longer corresponded to the prior commons. Non-corporeal scenery sometimes looks the same as its carnal semblance, especially if the dead person doesn't know he is dead.

And there isn't just here and there, life and afterlife. There are as many realities as representations and imaginalities in All That Is. These are inhabited, bardo after bardo, ghost to ghost, hunk by hunk—dust to dust. Because brains cannot store multiple lifetimes simultaneously, realities are cached in auras. Each effervescent village falls into cryptomnesia, beyond neurochemistry, occasionally twinkling back for a second or less before it fades again, for the aura is a far more fluctuating repository.

Décor is hidden like Edgar Allen Poe's purloined letter—in plain view: in minutiae of current lives, in hues of skies, in hexes and stuck and crossed karma, in interactions that carry covert meanings, in synchronicities and serendipities, in inexplicably arising agendas, in landscapes bleeding through congruent landscapes. Lives can be never *un*alike, so they mask each other like altered versions of the same photograph or script.

Something totally obvious is, ironically, not obvious at all.

The difficulty posed by suicide, if you believe in soul continuity, is not just the matter of a broken and lost life or a ruptured transition between bardos; it is the attempt to gain control of the projection. Once you lasso the thoughtform and then snap it by one or another vandal act, you forfeit a stable flow of karma and put yourself in a potential loop of recurring projections like weatherman Phil played by Bill Murray in the 1993 movie *Groundhog Day* in which February 2 kept recurring with different props and scenes from the same probability point.

If all phenomena arise from the mind, the issue is not whether a given reality is a dream or a "fact" but whether the dreamer creates the dream or the dream the dreamer. To get lucid dreaming confused with controlling a waking dream makes it difficult to unravel the riddle or set an anchor and fix an astrolabe.

Ghosts are life forms that are no longer alive—alive in a biological sense. They are entities in transition. "Ghost" *Geist/gast* is a proto-Indo-European phoneme with Paleolithic onomatopoeia: spirit, breath, anger, mind, soul. It was cried first by birds, monkeys, and cats, as they recognized a thing, a spook perhaps, perhaps after eating spirit berries. "Poltergeist" adds the Germanic *poltern,* "to make sound; to ring, roar, rattle, or rumble."

In M. Night Shyamalan's 1999 movie *The Sixth Sense,* Malcolm Crowe, a murdered psychiatrist played by Bruce Willis, takes on a child patient, Cole Sear, played by Haley Joel Osment. The child's "problem" is that he not only sees but is also importuned by dead people. Even while treating the boy and, at the same time, having no success getting his wife's attention, Crowe does not realize that he himself is dead.

A dazed spirit adapts every situation to suit his habitual reality and normalize a delusion. The living do it too. That's how the living and dead mingle without knowing it.

John Friedlander's teaching partner Gloria Hemsher, a highly attuned psychic, told me of awaking from anesthesia in a Boston hospital after hernia surgery. A bevy of dead folks rushed toward her because they knew she could see them. "It was exhausting," she said. "I needed to rest and recuperate, but I wanted to help them, guide them toward the light."

Salicrow, a necromancer with both Blackfoot and Druid ancestry and training, told me, "Mediums are like lighthouses. People flock to me because they can see me."

Ordinary folks are faint candles.

Buildings and other sites can become "haunted"—from the Old French and Middle English "a place visited frequently." Favored "haunts" include battlefields, sites of plane and car accidents, houses in which spirits lived when embodied, and graveyards—in principle any locale from a prior waking life.

Visitors to 9/11's burial ground reported seeing and/or hearing spirits of the slain chanting alongside their hijackers: suicide bombers, stockbrokers, and passengers, crooning in a dialect beyond all languages, in a zone that precedes bodies and ideologies—because they had no other choice and nothing else to do—not now, not any longer, not even then.[12]

The plot of *The Sixth Sense* involved getting spirits to go where their energy belonged—everything in the universe *belongs somewhere*. To that end, each soul goes in search of its own Atman—the sum of all its incarnations—a quest reinvigorated lifetime by lifetime.

Every ghost crosses into the light.

After my half-sister's death by suicide in 2016—she jumped from her eleventh-story window in New York City—her body stayed alive for about an hour, though her soul likely left on impact. In the days afterward, two occupants of her building experienced an identical haunting: an attack by hanging art. Others may have but didn't report it. A picture flew off the wall such that one of its corners hit each of them above the nose, just missing an eye, leaving swelling and a gash; in one case, needing eleven stitches. At the time, I wrote: "A piece had sheared from the unstable fusion of Deborah Towers. As a vortex of emotions, energies, and desires fissioned on stone, it sent out a series of waves, fractal sub-entities, one of which was drawn blindly and telekinetically to Parce."

That remnant—adoring, jealous, dislocated, desperate—wanted to be anything but itself. John Friedlander explained: "Poltergeists are debris from beings who have died with unresolved issues. They're thoughtforms. All their mobility is derivative. It's generated by someone who *was* a being. It came from your sister, but it was an empty thought-form without essence."[13]

Apparitions including most poltergeists are different from spirit visitations. Some apparitional poltergeists have a portion of essence, while others are *only* apparitional: stray energy, dybbuks that become thought-forms in psychoid interfaces with human projections onto them. We cannot always know if a spirit is a self-aware artifact of a deceased person or a lookalike deputized for an errand or unfinished task. Self-aware artifacts are visitations as opposed to mere apparitions.

UFOs, by the way, pose the same predicament.

In certain venues, a ghost earns an ectoplasmic shape, an activation of physical vapors by its spirit vapors. The boundary between the dead and living becomes charged with ethers that can injure or kill a live person on contact. UFOs likewise. Remember those twelve Russian airmen.

Other "ghosts" or spirits attach *intentionally* to living individuals, changing hosts from lifetime to lifetime, sometimes millennium to millennium, as they try to heal lesions: murders, jailings, betrayals, unrequited romances, gender dysphorias, unjust exclusions. By melding with incarnate folks in walk-in fashion, they convert desires and actions of a "zombie" to their own intent. This is the fare of witch-vampire kitsch.

Modernity may ignore or fantasticize spirits and poltergeists, but the oldest superpower of *Homo sapiens* is to cross interdimensional thresholds and rivers, mollify guard dogs (or canine psychoids), descend through caves between the living and the dead, *and return.*

At a few ticks before the one-hour mark of *Orphée,* time stops and Orpheus and Heurtebise enter a no-man's land between life and death. While Heurtebise is blown along motionlessly, Orpheus has to struggle to move. "It is different for me," Heurtebise says, for he is already dead.

Shirtless suspendered young men, panes of glass slotted in wooden holders strapped to bare backs, pass—first one, then another. *"Vitrier!"* they cry. *"Vitrier!"* They are, or were, glaziers.

An old man pushes a wheelbarrow-like wagon.

"Why are these people prowling around?" asks Marais in the English subtitles. "Are they alive?"

"They think so," says Heurtebise. "There's nothing more habit-forming than habit."

Orpheus stares in disbelief.

"Don't think I know," Heurtebise warns, "much more than you do."

Don't think that anyone here knows much about what is *actually* going on.

"There's no wind. Why do you always seem to be heading into the wind?"

"Porquoi," replies Heurtebise. *"Toujours porquoi."*[14]

So many questions, so few answers.

In Martin Scorsese's 1988 adaptation of Nikos Kazantzakis's novel *The Last Temptation of Christ,* Willem Dafoe as Jesus asks to be taken to the place where deceased Lazarus is entombed. A giant stone must be removed from a cave's opening, pried loose, and rolled away by extras, men and women with wooden poles. They hold their noses from the stench, Jesus too.

He stands at the opening and circulates his arms like a magician or *chi gung* master. On the soundtrack, voices warble and combine in many languages as if the portal to the afterlife were opening and all the souls and creatures who lived on earth were gathering and celebrating their current existences and coexistence itself in operatic mode. Consensus reality has dissolved into radical hermeneutics—what visitors heard and saw at the World Trade Center, an overlap of worlds and activated poltergeist energy.

In Scorsese's version of John 11, Christ summons Lazarus, "In the name of most Holy God, I call you here, Lazarus." Voice is used as mantra, voodoo, telepathic control. In Peter Weir's *Last Wave,* Australian Aborigine actor Nadjiwarra Amagula pulls off this feat more convincingly than Dafoe. When as a "songline shaman" he repeats a word and tone, it sounds like a buzzing bee. It hypnotizes, binds, and opens the Dreaming itself to the lawyer played by Richard Chamberlain. Suddenly even a fictive room doesn't look like a Hollywood set.

In Scorsese's cave tomb, Dafoe's Jesus reaches for Lazarus's dusty hand, strips of rotting flesh hanging off, pulls him up, and leads him out to the throng. The otherworldly chorus surges.

Lazarus reaches, slowly removes the death shroud from his face, and embraces Jesus. Jesus whispers, "God help me." For the miracle astonishes and scares him that the power that holds worlds intact answers to a son's beck. No one who is given such power ever wants to use it, except Jesus, and that is what made him the Christ.

In the testimony of John, Jesus's biblical persona says to Martha, "I am the resurrection, and the life: he that believeth in me, though he were dead, yet shall he live: And whosoever liveth and believeth in me shall never die."[15]

A mere miracle becomes a sacrament.

In Kazantzakis's version, Lazarus confides to Saul, "I like the light." Saul asks him, "What was it like? Which is better, life or death?"

Lazarus replies, "Well, I was a little surprised. There wasn't that much difference."[16]

That absence of difference is how Jesus kept his promise; it is also why death does not stay the dead from maintaining their worldly projections.

After the passing of poet Edward Dorn in 1999, his widow Jennie and daughter Maya experienced several lucid visitations. After a while, the "haunts" stopped but not before Ed bid Maya farewell, telling her that he was going to "another universe."[17]

Another universe! We would expect no less from a poet who wrote: *"The stars look very cold about the sky / And I have grown to love your local star / But now niños, it is time for me to go inside / I must catch the timetrain / The parabolas are in sympathy / But it grieves me in some slight way / because this has been such fine play / and I'll miss this marvellous accidentalism."*[18]

So may we all.

By the premise at hand, single lives are soul cinemas blown into bubbles that float through their own blue or yellow heavens before evaporating into brighter eternity. Then they are blown again. Mind and matter remain at par. Personae dissipate and return to the projector for the next mummery. Instead of a different movie, same viewer, or a different viewer, same movie, it is a different viewer, different movie, yet the viewer remains. Once again, amnesia is an effective form of encryption. It was never a zero-sum game of something or nothing; it was interdependent reality expressing itself *independently.*

Each sleeping giant, as large as a sun or as small as a beetle, awakes from Rip Van Winkle's doze, and says, "Okay, let's go. What am I now?"

"Oh shit!" Or "Oh wow!"

We have entry, exit, and a vision—anything else is copacetic. All we can ever be, anyway, is travelers between worlds.

In a final interview before his premature crossing from brain cancer, psychonaut Terence McKenna told *TechGnosis* author Erik Davis, "I always thought death would come on the freeway in a few horrifying moments, so you'd have no time to sort it out. Having months and months to look at it and think about it and talk to people and hear what they have to say, it's kind of a blessing. . . . I could see the light of eternity, à la William Blake, shining through every leaf. I mean, a bug walking across the ground moved me to tears."[19]

A ladybug or spider or chirping parula, a maple or the almond scent of white meadowsweet moves us to tears. A flock of passenger pigeons, a herd of wooly mammoths, a duck-billed platypus . . . a fabulously beautiful parade of stable ghosts.

A year earlier, McKenna told a San Francisco audience, "Every electron is the yawning mouth of a wormhole that leads to quadrillions of higher dimensional universes that are completely beyond rational apprehension. Matter is not lacking in magic. Matter *is* magic."[20]

John Friedlander grazed the big picture while locating his friend Will Ives who had committed suicide several years earlier:

I can say hello to Will now, even though there's no circle you can draw around Will. If you knew Will and you met this Will, you'd say, "Okay, that's Will."

The "Will" individual is now Will as something much more

complex and rich and kind and generous and yet knows itself as that—and is centered as that. Over subsequent years since the mid-90s, I started to notice more details or maybe Will spread out in more detail. When I see Will now, Will is centered in maybe five consciousnesses that I can perceive and have some sense of what they are. They are different personae of Will. Each one of them is as much Will as any other. And each one of them is fully engaged as that consciousness knowing itself simultaneously as each of the others.[21]

Whitley Strieber's deceased wife and coauthor, Anne, described souls, including his and hers, as nonphysical beings inserted into the river of time: "We're light. Light alive. This is the energy of objective love, the desire to be itself. . . . We're everywhere, but the light is undetectable."[22]

She adds with poignant precision: "I'm not Anne anymore. I'm me. But I always be Anne for you."[23] Her oversoul speaks as her ghost.

Consider those around you—partners, lovers, coworkers, children, parents. None of them is who they presently play or will play in the big picture, yet that is who they are to you now in this brief, indelible script. In some fashion, they will always be "Anne" or "Joe," as you will be "you" to yourself, through all subsequent amnesias and intimations.

Miranda as Prospero's daughter (words by Shakespeare) speaks the wonder of every indigo babe:* *"O brave new world, that has such people in it."*[24]

That brave must a world be, to exist at all. As Thornton Wilder concluded his 1927 Pulitzer Prize winning novel, *The Bridge of San Luis Rey,* "There is a land of the living and the land of the dead and the bridge is love, the only survival, the only meaning."[25]

That's what "Anne Strieber" was trying to tell her once husband. That is what every animal on earth is trying to tell us, in whatever way it can.

---

*Attuned at the indigo spectrum of the sixth, or third-eye, chakra.

THE SCAM OF THE BEING OF LIGHT

When I was in conversation with Ellias Lonsdale in May 2020, on Bluetooth during my first out-of-town drive since COVID-19 sheltering began, from Berkeley center to Rancho Strozzi an hour away (twice that because of road construction and a Friday commute), then sitting, us two, in Petaluma on a patio, friends of many decades talking dharma and the indestructibility of impermanence, as wind from the Pacific toward the valley surged through eucalyptus, pine, and oak—Ellias proposed something that I knew peripherally, in fact quite well, but had never fully grokked: that we are partly living on other worlds, worlds that are not here.

That doesn't mean—and here is the radical twist—that there is this reality, and then another, and another and another, and so on, a dotted line to infinity through a bardo multiverse. It means that this world is formed by others and becoming others, and we are too. There is no hop-skip-jump to another dimension or reality where we stay intact if amnesiac, while the paradigm starts fresh and proceeds on a different basis. Even as souls, we aren't capable of such a trip. Instead, we continue to make worlds as radically different from one another as thoughtforms can be, all *simultaneously* dancing the Great Dance.

Creatures have done this on Earth since pre-Cambrian epochs, hominids since the Pliocene, beings elsewhere since before the Milky Way. The outcomes locally speak to the essential fluidity and metamorphosis of reality within the same double helix—tube worm and trilobite, sea anemone and condor. This is a world becoming, which explains its deficits and miseries but also its beauty, joy, and grace, which continue to drive it forward, into unknown unknowns and paradigm-busting turns.

There are no goodbye-forever "past lives" as such, nor can time travel occur whereby we get to meet other ages of ourselves as someone else. Past lives, whether we remember them or not, are part of this existence and happening *currently*. That is why suicides can't skip a step and go to a next, reconditioned reality. You can't turn out the lights, or everything including the luminescence and sound. You can't just toss in your hand for another. Doing so may temporarily interrupt the flow, scrambling tags that connect realities, warping continua, but consciousness's thread cannot be snapped, it can only be temporally rendered unconscious. There is no getaway car.

I assume that damage from suicide can be repaired, time earned back, just not in the same way.

To infer that we can reality-hop is linear and dualistic and doesn't take into account the nature of the labyrinth we entered by agreeing to existence (if, in fact, "agreeing" is what we did). All the rest—the scenery—is a consequence. It is being sown into existence by the permanent seeds of every life form, stone, river, and mountain on earth, which have fused into one Dreamtime.

Beingness is not *apart from* what happens. It is *only* what happens.

That morning, I dreamed that I was tricking someone into looking for a lost castle or lost lifetime or lost something. Others were conspiring with me. The scam developed from within the dream. That is, I didn't know what we were doing; I only understood it as it elapsed.

I think that it began as a straightforward detective case with clues, then grew into a more elaborate affair. In a room or on a stage was a being of light doing amazing things, shape-changing, dancing, flowing into and out of herself. She was a laserlike plasma of water. I initially believed in her until I remembered that we were tricking our client, pretending that his lost castle—or family or cold case—was here, in her, and that she was real, which she wasn't. At that thought, she changed from being almost real to being part of the scam.

I knew that our mark was fooled and that we were about to move to the next phase of the sting, but then the being of light, who wasn't really a being of light, injured herself, and a quick replacement was essential, not to break the illusion. Stagehands and makeup artists hastily prepared an ordinary woman, rather short and nondescript, in an adjacent room, to take the place of the woman of light via conventional stage magic—hands and strobes working quicker than eyes. Her bare stubby legs were being wrapped in ace bandages. She was not a *light* being-of-light.

Our gull couldn't see that part of the preparation, because I, or we, kept him distracted, as we hastened him past the changing room.

I don't know what happened next or how it went down, only that I recognized I was in over my head and the real event had nothing to do with the thing that I was perpetrating. The trick was and had always been a giant disappointment, in my dream life and in my "life" life. More than that, it was a negation of everything I believed in. I was dreaming a mere façade of something really important—*really, really* important. My melodrama was intentionally, self-sabotagingly displaced.

In deciphering this dream, though dreams as bardos are intrinsically indecipherable, I identified the scam as the one played on me by my natal family in hiding the identity of my real father, not once but twice (at birth and at age nine), so that I didn't find out that my pa wasn't either my stepfather or father until after my mother's suicide when I was thirty—she jumped out the same window as my sister forty-one years later.

As I examined the dream more closely, I saw one scam after another, all through my childhood and my writing, teaching, and publishing careers. Within my supposedly cherished beliefs, I saw the scams and fantasies I had played on myself too. So what was real? Did anything count, for itself beyond duplicities?

It was *all* real, for I was not only the scammer and the person being scammed but the narrator and dreamer. *Clearly* there was a raconteur, or the story couldn't have changed from a detective plot to a being-of-light castle scam.

The narrator told the dreamer about the woman being wrapped in bandages and then how we got our victim past a stage he wasn't supposed to see. He kept changing the context and meaning of events, as the dreamer hastened to catch up and make the dream both decipherable and indecipherable, e.g., veridical.

At the same time, each sham or chicanery played on me was super-real. Conducting deceptions was conducting life. We each conduct life by tricking ourselves, by becoming the dupe of our tricks, siding with being tricked rather than with the tricking or trickster. We make the trick real, as we make the fantasy and illusion real. We have no *other* way to sustain reality.

This is how worlds get made and what worlds are—giant scams turned real by those who believe them—become them, narrate them, dream them, recount them.

The being of light was real because the plight of the world cannot be unpranked, and certainly not by us. In fact, our job is *not* to unprank it but to fall for the prank so fully that we make it absolute, as prankster as well as dupe, as raconteur likewise.

When Ellias told me (later in our conversation during my drive) about his former life in Atlantis and how his memories of Atlantis had guided him through this current world, I understood that he was making it up. It was a prank on himself, though it carried him from the Bronx to a college in Binghamton to a commune in Vermont, to a Waldorf academy outside Sacramento to founding a mystery school in Santa Cruz, to entering its mystery naked, in Kauai, the Big Island, Colorado, Oregon, Arizona, Utah, New Mexico. It never occurred to him to challenge the story, though it wasn't of this world and defied everything around him. Reality itself was a deranged landscape, and the people in it were all doing surreal things in various trances, *mise en scenes* masquerading as gun shops and balloon fairs, saddle tramps and street buskers. They were kidding themselves that they were exposing the scam, which is what scientific materialism is: an attempt to expose reality *as* reality, which loses the existential point.

Ellias's intention never waned or flagged; it only grew more certain. He continued to make it more and more real—the soul's code—not only for himself but thousands of others for whom he read star destinies. He is long past seeing the woman being wrapped in the second room. He saw her once, and that is the point, and the difference, and what makes a psychic a see-er. He was able to see her and be undeterred. He understands and rejects the trick.

I took the dream, at a difficult crossroads of myself and the world, when all was in doubt, as way to recognize the trick for what it is and, unlike my relatives (my half-brother killed himself too, with a knife) keep living. Donald Trump and countless imitators perform these tricks every day. Their scams have replaced an integrity of fact that, sadly, had already replaced itself with a narrative of appearances. Our mission, if we choose to accept it—and we did once—is to continue to believe in the being of light, to help her manifest without harm or dire injury, as the world. That is the only future, here or elsewhere, no matter how big or manifold the shopping mall qua multiverse qua climate crisis and garbage patch gets. She is All That Is.

A year later, having finally gotten out of Northern California and the smoke and crime, living in Bar Harbor's synchronicity sinkhole, I dreamed of a series of wrong turns or uncanny trains, taking me all the way from eastern Maine to Albuquerque where I debarked in Ellias's backyard. He was playing with an unknown child in front of an Albuquerque set. I called out, asking him to guess where I was because I was still in Bar Harbor though standing next to him. As he looked around in puzzlement, I thought, "He must realize that this is Albuquerque because that is where he is living now," but he didn't. He couldn't guess. I finally said, "I am in Albuquerque because you are seeing me."

When I told him the dream the next day, he commented on our altered world, "I know this will sound crazy, but the future has already happened. Because everyone is living in a past that is already gone, they don't see it. They think can restore the past by a vaccine."

I mentioned that teams were taking the court for the playoffs, for he is a one-time basketball player and fan as well as an Atlantean astrologer.

"That doesn't make it what's happening."

REINCARNATIONS

Ian Stevenson, a psychiatrist conducting paranormal research at the University of Virginia, collected three thousand or so case histories of children who recalled having been another person in a past life. For four decades, Stevenson traveled tens of thousands of miles, gathering and filing reincarnation data. Most of his children recalled near enough locales and chronologies for him to conduct real-time forensics. Landmarks, families, and associates were identified and, in many instances, brought into contact with their ostensible "reborn" member.

The proof of a greater reality was that they could meet without anomaly or distortion—nothing broke the unity of time zone or consciousness.

In remarkable instances, scars from injuries, diseases, and death wounds of a "past person" showed up as birthmarks in their reincarnates. A museum exhibit at the University of Virginia correlates death certificates and coronary pictures with photographs of birthmarks on many of Stevenson's subjects.[26]

Two American children, James Leininger and Ryan Hammonds, born, respectively, in San Francisco (1998) and Muskogee, Oklahoma (2005), remembered recent past lives as (Leininger) James Huston, Jr., a fighter pilot shot down off the coast of Japan near the end of World War II, and (Hammonds) Marty Martyn, a bit actor and agent in Hollywood who crossed in 1964. Their memories incontestably matched details from their past persons' lives: names, numbers, locales, careers, marriages, lovers, shipmates, children, adopted children, vehicle colors.

Hammonds put the matter quite poignantly, "Mom, you still don't get it, do you? I am not the same as the man in the picture on the outside, but on the inside I am still that man. You just can't see on the inside what I see."[27] And "Why would God let you get to be sixty-one and then make you come back as a baby?"[28]

It's not God's problem if future and past selves coexist interdependently.[29]

Plus, if time can be dilated by relativistic momentum or condensed so that an entire lifetime is remembered in moment-by-moment detail during a nonfatal car crash or a mountaineer's near-death freefall of a few seconds, then time is not a cosmic constant but a neural artifact, a transitional energy that can be shrunk or expanded endlessly inside temporal phenomenologies.

Fisherman Wendell Seavey recalled "leaving" a memorial service for another fisherman and finding himself over ocean in territory familiar to both. Coming invisibly out of a sky, his friend addressed him and thanked him for watching over his traps while he was sick.

"It was wonderful there," Wendell recalled. "I didn't want to go back, but Frank told me, 'You have to go, you're at my funeral.' When

I came back into my body, it felt like running smack into concrete or turning into stone. It was so dense it was painful, but not a second had passed. The pastor was speaking, and I hadn't missed a word."[30]

In his younger days, Wendell took numerous folks to sea to scatter loved ones' ashes. He reported instances of quantum entanglement: the sun coming out from behind clouds, a wind picking up at the exact moment of transfer from urn to water. Wendell read these as the spirit saying, "Thank you."

Ashes are not a remnant of a person—they are incinerated crystals of a biochemical warrant issued and replaced by progressive RNA and mitochondrial supply lines to ribosome factories—but they contain an aspect of superpositional energy. Rainbows forming after cremations of lamas speak to the universe that is. They don't need explanation or interpretation.

TIME

Vishnu, creator god, and Narada, storyteller god and musician, were walking and talking one day. Vishnu was a true deity, while Narada was a Vedic pundit, so he asked his illustrious companion for an explanation of "maya," the world illusion. Vishnu said that reality was just a fleck of a dream in Brahma's mind. Narada wanted more, but Vishnu was done.

A while hence, they passed a village seated in a valley below their trail. Vishnu asked Narada to go to one of the houses and fetch him a glass of water. Narada walked a serpentine mile and knocked on a door. It was opened by the most beautiful woman he had ever seen. When she invited him in, he didn't vacillate. Soon he was engaged in conversation with her and then her household. He forgot his errand and asked her father for her hand. The patriarch was honored to have such a legendary pundit as a son-in-law. For Narada, it was a flash of euphoria and world beauty. It came with a dowry: a piece of her patrilineage's land.

Narada was married in a town festival. He and his wife built a cottage, plowed and planted a farm. They raised crops, joined in the activities of the village. Narada forgot his practices and became a full-time householder. He helped raise a daughter, then another, then a son. The children were growing, the farm prospering. Narada and his wife were happy together; they were merchants, stewards, elders.

Then one morning the river rose and overflowed its banks. As streets flooded, neighbors spoke of a nuisance, maybe even a few deaths in the region, nothing out of the ordinary. Yet the current continued to grow until it engulfed fields and then the village itself catastrophically. The world turned on a proverbial dime like the arrival of an unannounced plague or tornado. It swept away Narada's children, each in turn, then pulled his wife from his desperate grasp. Weeping as he was carried along in the torrent, Narada tried to keep from drowning. He finally grabbed onto a giant rock and pulled himself up on it.

There was Vishnu. "I sent you a half hour ago for a glass of water. Now do you understand maya?"[31]

SEVEN
Practices

PHENOMENA AND PHENOMENOLOGY

Across the marquee of modernity runs a chyron saying, Life is Happenstance and Vain. It's all epiphenomena bred collaterally by gravity, heat, and their by-products on rotating spheres quoined in 3-D arcs on universal curvature. How these forces originate is anyone's guess.

In Stephen Hawking's rendition of Genesis, they exist *fundamentally,* without extrinsic predecession. There was no spirit hovering over a formless deep. *There was no spirit.* Time is an invention, a by-product of a big bang. The universe does not have to testify at its own trial or disclose accomplices or aliases. It doesn't actually exist.

Brains evolve, on Earth as elsewhere, under selective loads by chemico-molecular sift, like rubbing two sticks together or mixing mud and mineral salts. Consciousness is an exotic aberration kindled by proteins in agglutinating stacks that synapse and cascade under a principle called "the more the merrier," turning phenomena into phenomenology while producing a show for its marionettes. The ruse and hoax are quite real but meaningless—and terminal.

This is not only modernity's "follow the science, duh!" meme but its religion and law. Those who challenge it get quarantined with climate deniers, conspiracy theorists, racists, and sexists.

I know. I have had this debate with countless secular friends:

anarchist philosopher Murray Bookchin, astrophysicist Fred Haddock, anthropologist Terrence Deacon, feminist historian Donna Haraway, novelist Paul Auster and his novelist wife Siri Hustvedt. Murray believed in New Alchemy but not spirit; Fred listened to moons of Jupiter but eschewed UFOs. Donna blended with sheepdogs but not were-hounds; Paul created universes from dice and dreams of vertigo but not *naguals* and levitation. Siri excavated the brain and mind without the soul. Modernity was on their side, not mine.

Cosmologist Steven Weinberg delivers an empathic but sad sermon to the faithful:

> It is almost irresistible for humans to believe that we have some special relation to the universe, that human life is not just a more-or-less farcical outcome of a chain of accidents reaching back to the first three minutes, but that we were somehow built in from the beginning. . . . It is very hard to realize that this all is just a tiny part of an overwhelmingly hostile universe. It is even harder to realize that this present universe has evolved from an unspeakably unfamiliar early condition, and faces a future extinction of endless cold or intolerable heat. The more the universe seems comprehensible, the more it also seems pointless.[1]

Even those who (like Weinberg) don't want to be downbeat and depressed take it as their obligation—their "heart sutra"—to disenchant sentient beings. We are flimsy eggs in a rain forest and comet swarm.

Another cosmologist reviewing the book of a third cosmologist issued scientism's verdict on a travesty formerly assigned nonexistent goddesses and gods:

> Eventually the Milky Way galaxy will fall into a black hole. . . . [W]hen the universe is 100 trillion trillion trillion years old, protons, the building blocks of atoms, will dissolve out from under us, leaving space populated by a thin haze of lightweight electrons and a spittle of radiation.[2]

Spittle and haze. Down and dirty, and pass the biscuits, or did you hear from our friend Ralph lately?

The opposing view is that the universe is a diffraction of core luminosity in a plexus vaster and more seminal and dimensional than any extant cosmos; it encompasses All That Is, anywhere and under any conditions or determinations. The light within that illumines an eagle, mouse, or Hilma af Klimt is the ground of creation. That's why stones and stars, rivers and mountains, are innately conscious. *Everything is.*

In *Bottoming Out the Universe: Why There Is Something Rather Than Nothing,* I posed the two paradoxes that boggle any scientific theory of All That Is:

> Electron microscopes and cyclotrons discover no statutory source. Instead of bottoming, quarks and preons dissipate into energy, curvature, strings, quantum fields, whatever scientists choose to call it. Where physicists once thought to find bottom, there is none. Neither is there bottomlessness, just dissolution of form or transition to another mode of form.
>
> Post-Newtonian physics with its shape-shifting quarks is the physics of a mirage. Materialists know this, *but they don't believe it.*
>
> Second, consciousness that witnesses itself as consciousness does not fit any unified field theory of physics. I'm not saying that physicists don't get out the shoehorn and make it fit. I am saying they do.[3]

Later in the book, I ask materialism to explain how all this rigmarole got here:

> Why construct self-aware creatures and proxy habitats from incidental and spare parts? Why make blue jays, eels, and catfish out of mudcakes?
>
> I can see how a random whirligig might centrifuge atoms out of quantum scrap—maybe, maybe even forever. I get that formal and efficient causes can ricochet molecules, even without a primary "uncaused" cause, though *even* that seems extravagant and clunky.

What I *can't* see is how this entire temple complex with its priests, wishing wells, and gamelans was created by the equivalent of ping-pong balls bouncing into one another.

"Something" blows "nothing" out of the water by splitting the proposition into a teeming latency that underlies it. No entity could emerge from that depth unless it bottomed out at the same depth. No sentient being could exist in a universe unless it bottomed out *with that universe.* . . .

Mind arises from matter *because* matter was already arising from mind, not because a hundred monkeys typing away on their machines found Shakespeare. . . .

If a single particle that could fit on a pinhead (with room to spare) gave rise to this entire cosmos, it wasn't a mote and it wasn't just spat by an ogre void. It was a shadow, the kinetic umbra of an object of illimitable dimensions. . . .

The problem for physics is, *a universe that has consciousness in it is a conscious universe. Everything that isn't conscious is incipiently conscious.*[4]

Buddhist cosmology accepts a ground luminosity from Gautama's own Vedic heritage but brooks no duality—no me and you, mind and matter, self and other. Each life form has only an interim dualism. There is no crab or swan. There is only "is." Self is a delusion as well as a mirage, a bare lucidity shimmering briefly with effects. Mind is the cause and source of the effect: samsara *and* nirvana, life and death, land and sky, happiness and suffering, nonduality and duality, luminosity and darkness. How and why mind would commit such a breach and infraction is without ordinary explanation.

Many Buddhist scholars view duality as a correctable lesion. This entire brouhaha is a lapse or a misfire, a super self-deception, a wrong cosmic turn.

But, again, how? How does an entire cosmogenesis get off track and go dual? How does an ancillary defect turn into a Persian carpet of galaxies and life forms?

There's the rub: the arising of phenomenology as *both* matter and mind, of duality *in* nonduality. Why didn't All That Is stay a plump and plucky globule emanating joyously in timeless time? Why fragment into ceaseless subplots? Why all the debris and tchotchkes—the spawn of protons and electrons? Why an array of *"poor little sheep who have lost their way / baaa, baaa, baaa"*?[5] Why bardos and hell realms?

The world *cannot* be discounted as inferior or faux, a gaffe committed at a corporate level. It exists for a reason—even the adventitious non-reasons of science are rationales. *It must be accounted for.* It must be accounted for within a nondual framework that does not assign it solely to divine misjudgment, extended poor practice, polymorphous perversity, or Murphy's law.

It is not enough to say, "Just go deeper into your meditation and practices and dissolve all that duality; the phenomena as such don't matter." There is a reason we are having these experiences; it is not incidental, trivial, or wayward. All lives are rich, meaningful, and consequential. Furthermore, UFOs, spirits, angels, ghosts, and the like break with nonduality as well as physics. To dismiss them, as some Buddhist practitioners do, as deficient states and dissociated revenants does not respect their autonomy, mysteriousness, and complexity.

Gods don't make mistakes, but neither does nature: *gnascari* is "to be born."

Nor can gravity be an interloper or slacker; it is expressing *something far more profound than mass and motion.* It is flowing out of a nondual canopy.

In its backwash, every leopard or lizard is as committed as Plato or Xi Jinping or Sabrina Ionescu to personal sovereignty. Each ego, iguana or bird, tracker or day trader, is driven to defend its autonomy, not as a role but a stipulation. If that's a snafu or delusion, why or how? Who or what deluded it? Who started the joke, invited the being of light, and set whole world laughing? Certainly not the Bee Gees.

Nonduality may be the prime directive—in fact it is: enlightenment, permanent holiday, get me the fuck out of here!—but, first things first, how did we get in, and how many bardos must Dylan's wild duck swim before she gets to sleep in the sand?*

The universe cannot be an accident, a freeway pileup creating the autobahn of space-time. Its urgency and vividness can't be dismissed as ancillary effects or spill off. Our presence here cannot just be caprice or ignorance—capricious how and for what reason? ignorant of what? Reality is as wondrous and horrific and imperative as it already seems. *And it has to be accounted for.* The force conducting it must be logged against something, an account somewhere. You can't have this big a circus or mercado without spectators and customers.

Calling it an illusion or lesion doesn't account for the engine of reality and how tuned and mighty a machine it must be to generate so many powerful phanerons simultaneously. How could a universal driver just get turned on, and at this chunky an echelon and with a cosmos full of partisans, without being fully endowed and having sacred license to run? A neo-Buddhist model can't demote reality to just another neo-capitalist scam in order to bless its own mindfulness commodities; it has to respect the full veridical burst and proof. Buddha did.

In Dzogchen Buddhism—I can't be as precise or subtle here as the commentaries—this reality comes from nowhere but us: our nature, unknowing, unbliss; our tedium, dullness, discomfort, evervation, gross attachment, display, cloudedness, deluded mind, twisted mind; inhibition of what is free in nature, clinging, creating, activating and accumulating new karma. The way out is not protracted or limited to practitioners. It is to relax into *rigpa,* one's innate nature, and enjoy its lucent panoramic view. But that is arguably what life did by splitting nonduality into samsara and nirvana in the first place, leading to a descent. It was apparently as unavoidable as egg-laying monotremes, though the goal is to reverse it intentionally. Even then, the paradox

---

*As a Baby Boomer, I assumed that Bob Dylan's "Blowin' in the Wind" was familiar enough to cite indirectly, but my editor Hazel continued to note that she couldn't make head or tails out of the wild duck. In checking the lyrics, I found that I had committed a "mondegreen," a creation of a new meaning by a mishearing of lyrics. I had turned a "white dove" into a "wild duck" and its "sail" into a "swim." In fact, both must swim many dharmas before they get to the sand.

is not solved, but it couldn't be because it is the cardinal source of not only paradoxicalness but existence.[6]

Self is a witness witnessing the witness witnessing itself, and that is the difference—an uninvited witness. He or she (or "they") are not epiphenomenal kibitzers, or they wouldn't hold the claim check for a phenomenology they entered bearing. This goes for conscientious crows and octopuses, industrious otters and wasps, photosynthesizing horsetails, hawthorns, and leaf sheep.

* * *

A single model suits the evidence and reconciles all the contradictions: creation as a series of self-arising, self-authenticating thoughtforms. Each reality is a droplet from a dropper, a dream-like projection of the creatures perpetrating it. It displays as if on a starry stage and sometimes looks like an eruption into a void because the view is gazing into itself, and not only into itself but into a self-similar reflection—a superposed facsimile. The inner depth, the arts of Asdzą́ą́ Nádleehé, Changing Woman, and other indigenous deities ignite an outward Dreaming. Yet no matter how vast and celestial its heavens, how palpable and sensuous the crashing of seas on rocks and sting of cyclonic sand, phenomena are special effects, projections of information with means in a quantum flow of *all* universes.

Any other answer, high- or lowbrow, throws you back into the briar patch.

Universes look, feel, and smell like the real thing because they *are* the real thing, however we hypostatize "real." No reality is solider or sturdier. Each set of local vibrations and frequencies are as robust and convincing to their habitants as ours is to us. They are *as* "material" too, emanating at par.

Hominids marched from the Stone Age to the Iron Age to the Machine Age—buggies, airplanes, escalators, food processors—then to the internet and robots, without a hitch or hiccup. Hand axes and bronze pots became plastics and silicon drives with no discontinuities in elemental properties or logic. In a hypothetical universe of dust and heat effects, this kind of spree is outrageous; it transcends its own sci-fi zeal, as it transcends the scalar backdrop of scale. It behaves more like a Dreaming or thoughtform than real estate or a cosmic dump.

Cities couldn't arise from Paleolithic rites overnight because this isn't a *pure* thoughtform. Empirical mind had to work its way through constraints of infrastructure and rebar and the density of a Physical-Etheric landscape. It took millennia for thought to herd enough particle fields into mindstreams to make jets, elevators, and cell towers. In *Bottoming Out the Universe,* I wrote:

> A seemingly random distribution of molecules and their compounds, many of them located underground, became modifiable into everything *Homo sapiens* needed, from weapons and clothing to huts, vehicles, and eventually microscopes and computer networks. That speaks to either an uncanny ability to turn lemons into lemonade or an intrinsic relationship between mind and matter.[7]

We tend not to recognize how simultaneously profound and perfunctory civilization is.

In *Dark Pool of Light,* I made a distinction between atoms (quantum focal bits) and atomicities (their psychic nuclei), likewise between molecules and molecularities.[8] Atoms and molecules are denser forms of atomicities and molecularities, so they respond more slowly to thoughts. Yet *even they* bend over time to serve intentions directed at them. We live in a Stone Age metropolis.

In a universe made of molecules, it takes billions of Earth-Sol orbits and uncountable quadrillions of episodes in nature to achieve a landscape as zany and active as this. Yet there are as many civilizations as there are thoughtforms, flowing through eternity, carrying creatures along like corks in a cosmic Ganges.

All that elapses here, from egg-laying reptiles in a Cretaceous Epoch to Māori hakas in the Holocene to Arkansas auctions in the Anthropocene—sand-paintings and orchestras, children playing in puddles to narco-gangs, genocides, and weapons of mass destruction—

is predicated in All That Is, so it must appear in each of its Dreamings. Near the end of *Bottoming Out the Universe,* I concluded:

> What is happening is what *it looks like is happening.* Starry night is not only a mirage but *a perfect mirage*: a phantasmagoria by its ephemeral nature, a spell because of its prolongation, an altar because of its capacity for transference, and an inertial field so powerful that it drives more proximal fields and galaxies by its zodiac. The universe knows that. Of course, it doesn't—it simply *is,* which is a more profoundly bottoming-out state.
>
> The thoughtform visible through the Hubble telescope as myriad galaxies is being generated and transmuted this very moment by sentient beings, ourselves included; it is a residue of the creation and destruction of trillions of *tulpas* emanating from All That Is at the frequency and collective intelligence of spirits everywhere.
>
> If the universe were real, it would be exactly the same as it is, so it *is* real and looks exactly like this, but *in a totally other way.*[9]

The nondual realm needed duality to express the paradox and complexity of nonduality, to break the tension of timeless satori. This is an incredibly joyous and excruciating thing, but whoever put it here and us inside really nailed it.

BUDDHISM

Buddhism is the most meticulous, revelatory field theory we have on twenty-first century Earth. It addresses the brocade as well as the ontological biggies: latency and manifestation, viewer and view, individuation and dependent existence, illusion and veridicality, identity and impermanence, the causes of happiness and suffering.

There are many Buddhisms. In the aftermath of Gautama's life, variants emerged in Tibet, Japan, China, Thailand, Burma, Korea, India, Vietnam, Cambodia, Mongolia, and the West, each with its own flavor, practices, archive, and moral hierarchy—each a dipstick in the void. As Buddhism spread east, it merged with indigenous systems of magic and shamanism (Bonpo in Tibet, a Qormusta Tengri pantheon in Mongolia). It enlisted drums, sky devotions, divinations, *ovoos* (sacrificial mounds), *tulpas* (visualizations and altars), ancestral constellations, nature spirits, male and female intercessors, and peaceful and wrathful deities. Remember, wrathful deities are not intrinsically evil or revengeful; they are emanations of our deeper nature, guides through shadows, haunts, and clusterfucks of embodiment. Only a wrathful deity can get you past this much traffic and gridlock to the Great Mother.

By interrogating its own nature, Buddhist mind recognized that it cannot exist independently; it is dependent on not only everything else *but itself.* "Being" leads the parade, and there is a humongous gap between it and the other floats.

Most forms of Buddhism prioritize breaking the spell of phenomena—of mind-based projections—and re-rooting in a canopy of nondual clarity. The shift is accomplished through a series of meditations, body and mind purifications, prayers to deities, bows, chants, guided visualizations, mantras, gratitudes, offerings, and related *ngondros*—spell-breaking practices. Breaking the spell is the agenda.

Still, Buddhism is not a "users' guide" to the universe because there is no such guide or universe—no operating manual or operator. Manifestations present their own enigmas and challenges—the riddle will never be solved, the kōan clarified, because there is always another, and another: emptinesses becoming forms, dualities becoming differences. There is likewise no formulaic liberation and salvation. There is only a continuing inquiry into our own nature, a dialogue with the universe.

Buddha was not a Buddhist; Christ was not a Christian. Jesus entrained a Christic vibration and made Earth vibrate at its frequency, thereby become Christ the Lord. Gautama taught the Buddhic plane at a Sattvapatti frequency, thereby becoming the Buddha. An awakened prince, he shifted the frequency of Hinduism without altering its Vedic signal. Jesus of Galilee and Jerusalem, a renegade rabbi, transformed Jewish mystical practices by baptismal ablution and a new covenant, deepening Yahweh to encompass a wounded healer, a virgin goddess, and a holy ghost.

When Zen teacher Paul Weiss asked Tibetan lama Anam Thubten Rinpoche if he was a Buddhist, Thubten replied, "I'm not any form of 'ist; I'm a student of the dharma." He meant that he had motivation and conduct but no Buddha announcement or brand.

Buddhism exists because *we are already enlightened.* If 'twere were not so, Buddhism would not exist and we would not exist.[10] This is a tautology and paradox, but it is what must be accounted for.

In science's assay, reality is the source of its own illusion—a mirage of another mirage, reflected through molecules and microtubules. Buddhism looks to the mirages' arising—their source, not their medium. Where the Vipassana rendition of Hindu *maya* meets the world-illusion of physicists, it disseminates its ground luminosity into everything—everything material and everything imaginable: electrons, stars, clouds, mountains, oceans, birds, murals, desires, fairy tales.[11] For the Buddhist practitioner, the world may be an illusion, but it originates from something that is *not* an illusion. For the scientist, there is nothing that is not an illusion, a flow of electrons through neurons.

In Buddhism, the thoughtform constituting the universe—all universes—is rooted in the soil of the truth mystery: that is why we are here, or anything is here, and why we know and care about it.

For an orthodoxy-bound scientist, it's electrons generating epiphenomenal recognition.

Yet the contradictions that link life's many explanations and practices are parallel and reciprocal: one's surface functions continually as the other's depth—and *vice versa*—and so on, on and on, at every emerging tier as they continue to unfold through each other. Short of living in a monastery or a cave, we cannot escape the elucidation of raucous, raw phenomena. People must find shelter, eat, drink, and provide, but at no time does contemplation of the dharma cease, even at its raunchiest docks and truck stops, for all are created from the same *rigpa* essence.

Each state of self-awareness is filled with source luminosity 24/7 while conducting householding, gainful labor, social service, ritual chest-bumping, mating, and survival, for a moth or skunk too, for a sunflower. None of it requires a church or rectory, though some practices need the favorable conditions of a human birth. *Everything* is a student of the dharma, even a boulder in a field. Who is practicing the dharma *is* the dharma, so there are as many dharmas as practitioners.

The Zen initiate sits for hours, months, years, on a bench or zafu or rock, trying to tame reptile and monkey minds, to embrace the ground luminosity, disperse the illusion, and regain his or her fundamental dignity. But—and this is also how non-nondual reality gets accounted for—so do the bartender and back-hoe operator. Each is excavating an identical luminosity. Each is writing tablets on holy body-minds. And there is no operating manual otherwise.

Everything is doing zazen. A porcupine is doing zazen as it shuffles through the scrub of an exorbitant unwilding.

In a journal note, Buddhist poet Charles Stein, my high-school buddy, sifted this mud as unmuddledly as it can be strained:

> The single issue for me in Buddhist practice is the removal of "attachment" from cognitive commitments universally. This includes both thematically developed beliefs and continuously occurring spontaneous, athematic cognitive performances. Eliminate the whole cave of phantoms in a single gesture, and so forth.

He listed obstacles that are also opportunities:

> The "reality" of the external world (natural science), the reality of the inner world (psychology), the reality of consciousness itself (phenomenology, transcendental idealism, reduction of consciousness to neuro-physiological phenomena), the "linguistic turn(s)," the dependency of cognition on language in the sense of structural linguistics, the ontological primacy of language (Heidegger/Derrida, Lacan, say, or even the later Wittgenstein), the reification of essences, platonism(s), the primacy of "reason," of experience, of physical nature, of the forms of time and space, of logic as such, mathematics as such, of social/cultural/economic context, etc.
>
> Every philosophical position stands as an obstacle for Buddhist practice because precisely the principled terms of the methodology

of each threaten to capture the cognitive functioning of the individual in such a manner that the release from attachment to cognitive functioning itself is contra the order of the day. It is a displacement of the capacity for cognitive functioning from its absorption in such functioning's posits.[12]

He is saying, I think, that the practice of Buddhism is always the *next* obstacle in Buddhist practice. One progresses when that is recognized. Practicing Buddhism as if it were merely Buddhism—textual instructions—becomes Buddhistic obfuscation.

John Friedlander tells his students, "What's in the way *is* the way. *Not* what's *in* the way is *to be gotten out of the way.* What's *in* the way is your next spiritual step."[13] But only until the next thing gets in your way.

You can't also claim *"tired of livin'"* and/or *"fear'd of dyin'"* like "Old Man River." You have to push back with a warrior's heart and a dragon's spirit. As 1950s Yankee catcher Yogi Berra is rumored to have said, "If you come to a fork in the road, take it."

Stein continues:

The mind relaxes "in its own nature" as a current formulation in English has it. One awakens to instantaneous presence, pure awareness, in release from that of which it is aware—but without abandoning that of which it is aware, without abandoning its attunement with and from cognitive functioning itself.

He concludes:

I cannot countenance my own ignorance and dull-headedness or trust them to protect me from contemporary intellectual hyperclarity and inchoate, coercive cognitive miasmas.[14]

Chuck and I have been talking to each other since we met in 1959, so I accept the immaculacy of his attention as well as his refusal to be *bound* by immaculacy. I understood it in a different way when he was the star of the Horace Mann bowling team and we tossed a hardball between classes.

Another friend my age who is a lifelong Buddhist practitioner, an Idahoan I didn't meet until I was thirty when he became my *t'ai chi,* meditation, and food-as-consciousness teacher, trained himself to defer his personal will to the guidance of bodhisattvas. We are now more than twice that age, and he told me recently about a particularly painful meditation retreat in the Pacific Northwest, a hundred times more painful than the hard labor he performed on construction crews and in factories during his youth.

At the peak of discomfort, he experienced a thing he knew and suspected but never firsthand—the Original Splendor. Its radiance connected everything and everyone and had always been there, in charge and okay. He awakened to instantaneous presence and pure awareness.

A third Buddhist friend, ten years younger than me, a Minnesotan I met as a martial-arts teacher at my age forty-eight, heard me on a 2021 podcast and questioned my most recent revision of non-nondual primacy (I had ingenuously chirped, "This reality must be accounted for!") on the basis that suffering is unbroken, an existential hazard, hence always our ontological baseline. Those are my paraphrasings; Ron doesn't talk like that.

I agree with him—that's the paradox: any great truth becomes so only when its opposite is also true. Suffering must and can't be indemnified. Observe its primacy worldwide: hunger, slavery, disease, imprisonment, torture, fire, floods, earthquakes, drought, predators; depression, addiction, psychosis, terror, old age, death. Ron put it in a cozy nutshell:

> Your view of enlightenment seems a bit off. It isn't a self-oriented goal, at least in the Mahayana traditions. It isn't a state to be attained. The goal is to realize the causes and conditions of suffering, and Buddhism offers a path to stop creating those causes and conditions. If we can do that, enlightenment is the result. The seed of Buddhahood is in all sentient beings, veiled and obscured but always there. Purifying those

veils, not creating any more, cultivating virtue, subduing the mind—those are the teachings of the Buddha.[15]

He reminded me, as he did often on the mat, we don't have the luxury of accounting, or even thinking, when the tiger's leap, bear's hug, or eagle's claw is headed our way. Especially when we co-create the tigers. One encounter, one chance; karate and creation.

By the same measures, I hold the Spirit Rock Meditation Center in Woodacre, outside San Francisco, in high regard for its transmission of the dharma by wise, straightforward teachers like Jack Kornfield, Philip Moffat, Tara Brach, Pema Chödrön. Yet when I attended a memorial service there in the late nineties for Rick Fields—a Buddhist historian, journalist, and long-time friend—the Buddhist poet Joanne Kyger, the center's near neighbor in Bolinas, called it "suburban Buddhism." She added, as we entered the grounds, "Are you ready for the Sunday shamans?"

She meant that Buddhism was her resumé and garden. Years earlier, she wrote, *"There is something in me which is not open, it does not wish to live / it is dying."* There is a thing in each of us, which cannot be claimed, redeemed, sat, out-sat, earned by merits, or granted by a teacher. *"But then in the sun, looking out to sea / center upon center unfold, lotus petals, the / boundless waves of bliss."*[16]

You can't cede that to Buddhist seniority. Buddhism may set enlightenment as both its explicit and implicit goal but, remember, this reality was propagated by *an already enlightened* intelligence. That's why the flaw is not a flaw.

I have no issue with Buddhism. I honor its many forms and sects. My issue is with practitioners who presume that they hold the operating manual for the universe and then count retreats as steps on the path to enlightenment like papal indulgences. By sanctifying abstinence, they hope to earn moral authority over the misery, shambles, and freight trains of distraction. By sitting, they hope to get out of the shitpile and transcend its *merde*. Would that there were such a guidebook and shitpile!

The problem is not with Buddhism or the dharma; the problem is with mindsets of capitalism-dominated polities: commoditize everything, even nonattachment.

Paul Weiss made good-natured fun of this inclination, including his own susceptibility to it, by rewriting the "crooked man's" nursery rhyme:

There was a Buddhist man, and he walked a Buddhist mile,
He found a Buddhist sixpence against a Buddhist stile;
He bought a Buddhist cat which caught a Buddhist mouse,
And they all lived together in a little Buddhist house.

EXERCISES

For Ms. Kyger, who journeyed in India and Japan, doe-eyed out of suburban Illinois, poems were meditations. For lyricists like Sappho, John Donne, John Keats, William Blake, W. B. Yeats, Edward Dorn, Diane di Prima, Mary Oliver, Joanne, and her Asian traveling buddy, Gary Snyder, they were prayers, mantras that illuminated their own souls and those of others, guiding us into mystery realms.

My first "exercise" is to take in poems—not existential, socially decorative verses but transmissions. Read poets who use language to address mortals as they would gods, because they are addressing gods too. In "Asphodel," William Carlos Williams wrote: *"It is difficult / to get the news from poems / yet men die miserably every day / for lack / of what is found there."*[17] As a doctor, he meant it literally: spirit medicine.

Read any Dzogchen or Zen text. Tsoknyi Rinpoche, Namkhai Norbu, Chögyal Trungpa, Shunryu Suzuki are among my favorite authors—you don't write this stuff unless you've lived it. Read the Seth channelings of Jane Roberts (because they come from another dimension); the Gurdjieff lineage (particularly P. D. Ouspensky and Rodney Collin, because they bear a proto-Indo-European dharma); Rudolf Steiner's anthroposophy (where the soul descending meets matter arising); the Sufi precepts and guided visualizations of Hazrat Inayat-Khan and his son Pir Vilayat-Khan and *his* son Pir Zia-Khan; Andrew Harvey's *Way of Passion* as a firewalk through Sufi Jalāl al-Dīn Rūmī's ecstatic flames; *Navaho Religion* by Gladys Reichard for its sandpainting sigils and soul-retrieval ceremonies; the Osage Rite of Vigil translated by Francis La Flesche (because vigil is a rite that, if not practiced sincerely, leads to vigilance and vigilantes); Carl Jung's *Psychology and Alchemy, Symbols of Transformation,* and *Archetypes of the Collective Unconscious;* and the Christian Apocrypha. Make your own list.

I reconstructed the following exercises from a variety of sources; they are my own current mainstays.

Finding the Soul

Choose an event from your life, significant or incidental. Note its nuances, subtexts, overtones, unexplored reaches. Ask if it is imbedded in more than one lifetime. To what is it tethered? In what is it moored?

Ask the self that asks the self until it dissolves into waves of being-ness. Keep asking and accept any answer. Let the unseen realm remain senior, senior to everything you know or think you know. Let it soften, expand. Let the sound of an automobile or crow or voice in the distance or tinnitus enhance the meditation: How came ye to be in a sea of stars?

Go back to the initial self and relight its pilot. Can it disperse like smoke and return to form?

Who *are* you? What is creating mind? Is it creating itself? How? Can you find its unfabricated translucent source?

Where Am I?

Feel the silent static of other worlds, realms, sanghas, domains, dimensions. The quieter you are, the more of them manifest like a din of crickets. They are part of this incarnation too.

For Sleep and Waking (Paul Weiss)

Be the body. Don't *feel* the body—*be* the body. By being the body, you become the soul.

Paul's mnemonic device is SE(X)Y: Still, Empty, Silent, Complete, Yes! I will add William Blake: "Man has no Body distinct from his Soul;

for that called Body is a portion of Soul discerned by the five Senses, the chief inlets of Soul in this age."[18]

Preventing or Lessening Trauma (Michael A. Singer)

Whatever you are hiding from, let it in. To the extent that you try to block or override a fear or concern, it will grow in omneity and influence, augmenting its stake in you, claiming more and more of your freedom until you become its prisoner:

> [A]ny behavior pattern based upon the avoidance of pain becomes a doorway to the pain itself. . . . As long as you are afraid of the pain, you will try to protect yourself from it. . . . Once you close it, your mind will build an entire psychological structure around your closed energy. . . . If you close around the pain and stop it from passing through, it will stay in you. . . . Do you actually think that if you resist it, it will go away. . . ? Eventually you will understand that there is an ocean of love behind all of this fear and pain.[19]

Drinking Your Own Nectar (Heidi Hanson)

Triturate your essence: your ungrieved griefs, anxieties, regrets, déjà vus. Let them seep in. Assimilate them, dram by dram. Everything that is bane or enemy or nightmare is a source of power and awakening. Avoiding trauma is what turns trauma into PTSD.

No Instructions, No Cues, No Source (Heraclitus)

"The oracle whose lord is at Delphi neither speaks nor conceals but gives signs."[20]

The sign is not what you think. If it were, you wouldn't be consulting an oracle. Only the train that goes to the wrong station takes you where you need to be.

Mind and Sky (Paul Weiss, Buddhist sky meditation)

Set the bigness of your mind in the bigness of sky. Set both sky and mind *in the bigness that holds them*. Set those in your heart, the only engine deep enough to run them. Reach to the edge of the universe and let fresh golden energy flow from there down your crown into the *nadis* of your body-mind.

Opening the Physical, Emotional, and Spiritual Heart (Alexandra Whitney)

Feel the heart as a biological and emotional organ. Make your heart over from endodermal and mesodermal tissues; go where they meet, fold, and coalesce, left of center in the chest's cavity like two rivers joining.

As the mammal blastula differentiates, the heart is the first organ to form, a congealed spiral of interweaving streams imbued with life force—a primeval head and ego-self beating twenty-one days after conception. The heart carries the soul from the astral through the etheric into biogenesis.

Support the heart's functions by visualizing them: circulation of oxygen to cells, disposal of waste gases, stimulation of immune functions, communication among neural and hormonal networks. The heart governs the inspir and expir of each organ. Each heartbeat sends a complex array of signals to the brain and, to some degree, every tissue, charging emotion, perception, and the ability to reason and make choices.

Feel the heart's negative capability. If you perceive it only as an organ of love, compassion, and gratitude, you block its capacity to mediate and unify. The heart's regulation of parasympathetic and sympathetic nervous systems rests on a dynamic interchange between positive and negative stimulation: yin-yang, love-hate, euphoria-dysphoria, creation-destruction. Negative aspects trigger a stress response and fight-or-flight chemistry; positive feelings inspire synapsing and transform emotions.

The reggae beat simulates the heart. Band leader Ed Mondazzi told me that: its back thump, one-drop, and steppers match the rhythm of breath and blood.

Explore the sound's heartfulness, banter, epiphany, soul, sorrow—its positive-negative interchange: Max Romeo, "Jamaica Ska"; Bob Marley, "Corner Stone" and "Trenchtown Rock"; Israel Vibration,

"Rude Boy Shufflin'"; Gregory Isaacs, "Don't Let Me Suffer"; John Holt, "Why Do You Hurt Me So" and "Up Park Camp"; Lee "Scratch" Perry, "Django Shoots First"; the Skatalites, "From Russia with Love" and "Trip to Mars"; Yellowman, "Nobody Move"; Apache Indian, "Om Numah Shivaya."

During childbirth and lactation, the heart makes oxytocin in portions equal to the brain. This hormone activates cognition, tolerance, adaptation, sexual and maternal intimacy, social cues, and the development of human bonding, trust, and enduring relationships.

Put your heart on the scales of your mind. An average human heart weighs ten ounces and beats a hundred thousand times a day, forty million times a year, three billion times in eighty years—*almost* Uranus return. The heart pumps two gallons of blood per minute, a hundred gallons per hour, which travel through blood vessels and arteries that, if combined, cover sixty thousand miles, more than twice the circumference of the Earth.

The heart was once an independent living creature. It is reconstructed from a medley of invertebrates that swam for their food. It is beating not to keep you alive but because it is still swimming and feeding.

Send enzymes, hormones, and nutrients through your heart into your bloodstream; raise their fuel grade to *prana*.

The Western medical model limits the heart to its mechanical functions, so cardiologists are taught to view it as a muscle whose singular purpose is to pump blood. Yet case studies from patients indicate that an imported heart carries cellular memories and personality traits of its donor after transplant surgery. Part of the donor's energy field and life goes with the organ to the recipient.

Psychics knew this before cardiologists.

The heart is "the voice that speaks for the soul—the center of intuitive intelligence and of infinite emotional knowledge . . . the place where love lives."[21] The Buddhist canon refers to an "awakened heart" as *bodhicitta*. *Citta* means both "mind" and "heart," *bodhi* means "awake," "enlightened," or "completely open." *Bodhicitta* is also the feeling of a broken heart: "a place as vulnerable and tender as an open wound."[22]

Cardiac softness is the doorway to compassion: Understand the suffering of others through the vulnerability and goodness of your own heart. Be aware when the gate closes. Don't force it open. *Let* it open.

Buddhist nun and author Pema Chödrön said that "*bodhicitta* is capable of transforming the hardest of hearts and the most prejudiced and fearful of minds" and that everyone has this ability to love, "even the cruelest people have this soft spot. Even the most vicious animals love their offspring."

"When you touch your heart or let your heart be touched, you discover that it's bottomless, that it doesn't have any resolution, that this heart is huge, vast, and limitless. You begin to discover how much warmth and gentleness is there, as well as how much space."[23]

INITIATION

From childhood I have practiced a few basic forms with enough commitment to claim snippets of mastery. My skills are free association and dream interpretation (starting in psychotherapy at age eight), tarot reading (age sixteen), archetypes and symbols of transformation (twenty), *t'ai chi ch'uan* (twenty-eight), bioenergetics (thirty), craniosacral therapy (forty-four), and psychic healing (sixty-four).

I count a few secular practices at the same level: playing outfield in baseball, writing, academic anthropology, speedskating, publishing, domestic partnering, child-rearing.

At a lesser degree of engagement, often briefly, I have practiced Korean Zen, Vipassana, homeopathic repertorizing, astrology, shiatsu, rebirthing, contact improv, the Bates method, Continuum, yoga, *chi gung,* somatic experiencing, family constellations, and the crystal path (e.g., communication with stones).

At times of crisis and transition, *none* of the above served as a catch basin. They didn't get under my confusion, terror, or pain. They felt like borrowed coutures, artificial limbs. But that didn't detract from their import or the value I gained from having devoted myself to each in its moment. Maybe I didn't do any of the formal practices fully enough to get past its tipping point, but I moved at the rhythm and speed of my nature and the planets of my birth chart. And I used what they turned into in me.

If I had committed myself only to practices and exercises, I would have been searching forever for a nonexistent resolution, in therapy sessions and classes, at retreats and workshops, and by deepening my most advanced arts, hoping to get bailed out by one or another teacher or healer or leveraging my practices to bail myself.

Here's the thing: I tried and abandoned each of my more advanced psychospiritual skills during an 850-day depression (mid-June 2018 to October 20, 2020). I drew on their implicit spiritual agreements, called in their promises, and tried to milk or prise an escape from pain, a shift toward clarity and calm.

My techniques confirmed my apprenticeships, but they failed in moving depression's needle. Each time I found the path, I lost it. I lacked something crucial I once had: commitment, morale, ballast. I could create space and enter esoteric zones, but they were junior to the entanglements of karma and torpor of creation. What was left was winging it, the way people wing whole lives.

Only then did I draw on my lessons' *actual* assimilation and intelligence. I received a hermetic download that belonged to no system or method. It rang with past lives, serendipities, intimations, wonder and awe—whatever those are. It was like a psychic zip file that took me more than two years to download and assimilate. In the process, I found out what each of my practices really were.

If I had *only* winged it from the get-go like my more political and jock friends, I wouldn't have found a way or made it out. I needed the alchemy of successive baths.

Such a thing, this reality is—a pleasure palace and mirage. I was a fully committed participant once, in fact for a *very* long time. The long-ago-bulldozed swimming pool and buffet at my father's hotel, the summer-camp ballfields, the Long Beach surf, the makeshift tavern in Phi Psi's basement, the Roaring Fork River with a million Colorado stars, Vermont skinny-dipping holes, Bay Area bike trails, Hawaiian orchards and beaches, each a savor, were long gone, gone with Samuel Butler's way of all flesh.

In college spring 1964, I wrote:

One Saturday Larry drove us to a swimming hole north near Vermont: Jim, Schuy, me, and our dates. I felt an ancient wistfulness, as Lindy and I lay on our backs in bathing suits in the grass . . . clouds blown apart in the jetstream. I was chasing the bare eclipse of a form, itself a shadow. Beyond the hill, the land dipped precipitously into the unknown, an obliquity that masked a chimera. Something indelible was lost; something equally remote beckoned. I saw on a smoke-thin arras a Sphinx. I felt my own skeletal existence.[24]

That summer, I sensed it again:

In August, Mitchell led us to Snowmass to watch Trappist monks chant sunrise, a ceremony so profound and primordial that it hurt—it was deeper than I could bear. I would see that dawn again in coming years, sometimes recognizing it, sometimes sliding into nearer salves, for it held many mysteries in its fading arras of night. It would take fifty-five years for me to recognize *what it was*.

In September 2018, somatic-experiencing teacher Laura Regalbuto explained my depression this way, "What does an insect do when it comes out of a cocoon? It feels and rubs itself all over with its legs. It doesn't know yet what it is. It has to discover its body all over again."

I did, but not right away. It took me an additional two-plus years of dissociation and insomnia.

Necromancer Salicrow gave her own prognosis, "Your mother made this pact with you before you were born. Honoring it is what got you here. Now you are trying to break the weight of her karma, and that's a lifetime's work if you're lucky. Pray to any god you know. There is no way around this, only through it."

You don't change by doing exercises—laps, Pilates, conscious breathing, crunches, downward dogs, I-am-loving-kindnesses—you change by the willingness to change core intention.

Of course, you *do* change by exercises. Every *asana* is a *terma*—a prompt planted by your guides or unconscious mind, found when needed.

But there is no shortcut, no deluxe ticket, no workaround, no alternate way to cross a desert, abyss, or galaxy, no wormhole from one comfort zone to another. The path is inviolable.

You can't force-feed or *train existence*. You have to live it—whimsy, muck, murk, melancholy, fragile euphorias, nostalgias, regrets, chagrin, grasping, and the rest. You can't avoid the darkness of the soul; it's how you got born. When you try to stay in the light, you lose the teachings of the shadow; then you lose the light. You have to swim the lake, feel the cold and slosh of its water, know that you won't necessarily survive.

Because unless you are practicing intention from first glimmer like a lama or through sitting in an anchorite's cell, you can't solve life by techniques; you need maturation of soul. Practice is a default state. Its exit stability is your actual stability, the measure of your freedom. It is also your fallback, the realization that confidence holds (or doesn't) as it is jarred by disturbances, bad conditions, and adversity. Otherwise, the exercises are lip service posing as merits. Clarity grows by however many seconds or minutes of awareness, resilience, and compassion you accrue through life. Some hurdles are insurmountable and can't be trained or meditated away. They belong to the soul and must be accounted for, like reality itself, on their own terms. Insurmountable hurdles are the biggest unindicted cause of failed spiritual practices.

When I put together a book of lessons from John Friedlander's classes, transcribing single passages and exchanges from hundreds of hours of his teaching over a decade, I was searching for a particular exchange with a student. I had heard it on an audio download before I began the project. Finding it was how I knew when my work was done (even as hearing it cued me to start the project six years earlier).

On November 1, 2019, in a motel room in San Luis Obispo en route from Berkeley to LA, I found it, a gem of a response to a student's pique about how difficult she found her practice under adverse conditions. Here is a section from John's *Recentering Seth:*

You can't demand, "Beyond this line, life cannot go." You can say, "I really really really want to be able to get through this and be happy," but you cannot say, "Because I have a strong will power, I will always be able to do this." You have to engage that as a real experience, and the odds are overwhelming that you will be able to do it, but it will take however long it takes and, if you insist on it going faster, sometimes that will work because you have a strong enough will power, but if you don't deal with the underlying issues, sooner or later the issues will get more powerful than your will power, no matter how powerful your will power is. 'Cause your will power is set up to help you engage the world, not to put up a dam between you and what you consider to be unacceptable. . . .

You don't get to say, "I'm willing for the world to be chaotic but only *this* chaotic." You don't get to say how many issues are connected. . . . If you insist that it be what you're willing to put up with—I put up with fifteen different things, I shouldn't have to put up with a sixteenth—you don't get to engage this with a curiosity that leads to a kind of enjoyment.[25]

I'm just a transcriber here, so I'm no one to preach. I haven't trained *anything* fully, even John's system. I have ignored or abandoned every extolled guru graciously offered me.

In March 2019, I saw a shaman in Portola Valley, a Sunday shaman but a shaman all the same. Susan performed soul retrieval. As I lay on a table, she chanted, hummed, sang, drummed, played a flute, and made spirit-empowered water for me to sip, then swallow. She led me to a spirit leopard, and, afterward, reported what various entities revealed about my soul's path. I was being called, she said, to heal my lineage, my ancestors as well as descendants. "You're at the crossroads, but you volunteered to do this."

Whatever I believed about entities, sourcing, and planes, her message, without knowing anything about me or my other mediums and mentors, was pretty much what Salicrow, Ellias Lonsdale, and John Friedlander had said. John reminded me that this wasn't something happening to me; it was an agreement I made. He added wryly, "Just think. You may be saving yourself twenty or thirty lifetimes."

When Susan asked if I had any questions, I had one, "Is this unusual or typical?"

"I've seen it before, but most people have interference from intruding energies or their soul is wavering. You've got a bright soul but a difficult mission. In fact, your soul's been hanging outside your body your whole life like a feather attached by a strand, but you're starting to let it in. It was too dangerous before."

I had consulted a shaman in Maine before going west. She was trained in a different lineage but said a connected thing: "Joy is trying to reach you, but you have to pull your entire lineage along." The transmission was consistent, but was it spirit communication or a generic shaman-institute message?

When I told Ellias that I felt like a walk-in in my own body, he replied, "The other guy was a walk-in. This is you."

On an afternoon two weeks later in an Airbnb house, I tried to dissolve despair with a Rebirthing breath cycle, smoothing each exhale into the next inhale, affirming that, despite everything, I was where I needed to be. I thanked the universe for bringing me there.

Then I made a stopgap zafu from cushions and sat half lotus, letting my discomfort seep through my body-mind for ten interminable minutes.

I fled zazen and lay on the bed, eliciting the micromovements of Continuum, letting them extend, squiggle by squiggle, into a squirmy dance, crawling along the couch over its arms like an abalone. I prowled as a leopard around the room.

There was something huge missing. Was it love, joy, faith, engagement, hope, God? I wasn't drawn into anything. I was just me, faking, mimicking, longing, counting the seconds till I could try something else.

Using Feldenkrais techniques I had been practicing for twenty-five years, I swivelled head, shoulders, and pelvis, in differentiated arcs, separating eyes and spine, hips and arms. I circled head and eyes in opposing clockwise and counterclockwise directions, then lay on the bed, placed my hand under the back of my skull, and lightly followed and induced, then supported biodynamic waves. As they dissipated, I tuned my frequency to the Etheric field and rose to its bounty of creationary energy.

The splurge, intense and attuned, faded like the rest.

I stood in the center of the room and did *chi gung,* segueing its free-lance choreography into my whole *t'ai chi* set. My mind rushed ahead into Needle and Fan, Monkey and Snake, anticipating their payoff. I kept trying to bring my mind back to the move at hand.

I switched to Peter Levine's somatic experiencing, pendulating my despair between my torso where it throbbed and my fingers and toes, which received it as neutral energy. I chanted his "vus." The vibration of vuuu-shaped air changed my bones through my throat into my eye orbits and skull as if going from an oboe to a saxophone. It opened my embryonic channel to trauma trapped inside. But I could no more flush or regurgitate the vortex than I could vomit out the lining of my cells during motion sickness.

I cleared energetic pictures and cords from my aura and flushed its field by drawing fresh cosmic energy down through my crown. I filled my *nadis* with its golden light. Depression remained senior. I walked to the window and did a magical protection ritual conferred by psychic guide Steve Lumiere. I called protection angels by name. I set a radiant shield star around myself. I visualized sigils and asked for peace, free-dom, and the right to create my own life and immortality. *Totally and completely. Now and forever.*

Nothing stuck or stayed.

I plopped on the couch and stared blankly out the window. Only "I" was left, the same self that sat by a window, age eleven, at 1235 Park Avenue, looking down at 96th Street.

I remembered *tonglen.* With each inhale, I quietly took in the uni-verse's pain and suffering, from as far out as I could reach and as deep into my heart as I could go. With each out-breath, I sent compassion and love from the energy field of the organ to all sentient beings. In between the breaths, I conducted imaginal transmutation.

I wanted the impossible: to return to the old planet, to be young again, back when I was writing *The Night Sky* and *Embryogenesis,* planting rows of herbs, parenting a boy and a girl, learning a *t'ai chi* set, celebrating the Mets' 1986 comebacks when baseball still mattered.

While I was dawdling, killing time, light and opportunity were whipping by with the solar wind.

A swarm of gnats danced in a repeating mathematical pattern, rising and falling outside the window. Beyond, sun glistened on the tops of buildings and from the snaking BART along the sparkle of the Bay. I felt the start of possibility in something undeemed and unknown, emerging from nowhere. I tried to keep its spark alive, like a bashful fire in kindling. It would take 599 more days for it to catch.

The tendency of mind to steal from soul, light to steal from darkness, burgher to steal from warrior, impresario to steal from guide, guru to steal from his own beginner's mind is what stalls a technique in the technique's façade. We spend much of our lives seeking liberation in scabs of sublimation, proselytization, and the sheer static of transmission. My teacher Ron Sieh put it well on the mat in 1992:

> To progress at something like *t'ai chi* isn't hard because the techniques are difficult to enact. That problem is surmountable. What is hard is to wake up and stay awake, to sustain intention and keep doing it, especially after you mess up. You have to avoid distractions, especially the deadliest of all, self-sabotage, "What a fuck-up I am!" Because you try to make up for being a fuck-up by disowning your mistakes. No good.
>
> No error, no correction; no correction, no progress! Own your errors as a necessary phase. . . . You want to prepare to die consciously, your last breath awake and aware.

He also said, "I'm trying to teach you to be the best you can, but you obviously have some other agenda."

You don't have to be adept at Dzogchen to realize that the most crucial practice is the one you are doing every second. Ron was a Dzogchen dude too. He described his method as "A bit of hoitie-toitie Dzogchen, then some Tibetan voodoo. Tantra starts where sutra ends." He added, "I address this stuff by doing prostrations, chanting a mantra and thinking of, say, all the times I've hurt people, all the times I've caused pain to others, all the times I've tricked myself, *and then I burn it off.*" As he spoke, his hands rolled like a river.

He wasn't trying to get me to do *his* practice; he was trying to get me to find my own. His lesson was: if you're not training the good stuff, stability and all, you're training the bad stuff, grasping and envy habits. If you aren't listing toward *rigpa,* just a little, then you are creating obstacles at more or less the same frequency.

"Double-weighted," he declared. "No good. Double weight means you don't know who you are, you're taking your identity from your opponent, or your lover—same thing." He stopped and gave me his "here comes an aphorism" look. "The more control I have over my own experience, the less damage I do to myself and others. It's the people closest to me who have the potential to hurt me the most. The double meaning here is intentional." He shot a quick left hook. "Good deflection, but don't go away. Stay with it. It's not over. Here comes something else! Wham! The right!"

Later, he summarized, "You might as well start training this stuff because you're training something. You're training what you've always trained: sloppy habits, monkey mind. You've been getting better and better at them. Better at fear, better at self-sabotage. You're *already* training *in*attention. You're training *im*precision, distraction, all the time and very well. Why not experiment?"

He looked for acknowledgment, but I was transfixed by his words. He clicked two fingers in front of my eyes. "I am trying to wake you up, give you an art you can practice consciously at any time, get you to use your intellect instead of setting it in your way. . . . Be creative, for chrissakes. You're a smart guy. Draw the obvious conclusions. Don't stand there like a dufus, waiting for instructions. Invent yourself! Then invent yourself again."

So simple and straightforward. Yet so elusive. Where the mind emptying itself of itself meets the third eye of imagination, each must bow to the heart, to earn permission of the other. Twenty-eight years later I was still bowing.

In September 2020 during the first wave of the coronavirus pandemic, my wife Lindy and I left Berkeley and came to Bar Harbor to live, fifty-one years after we first crossed the Thompson Island causeway onto Mount Desert Island to rent a cottage on Indian Point Road. Later in that long-ago year (1969) we returned with five cats and a newborn son. I began interviewing fishermen, conducting ethnography for a thesis.

We returned to Mount Desert in 1996, eight years after empty nest, bought a farmhouse in Manset, and began spending four or five months a year downeast.

I had grown up in seasons but never noticed how branches come to life in April, dormant wood sprouts shades of green: leaves and buds. I took their magic for granted. Four decades in Cali made it seem witchcraft. After snowbanks shrank into mud—crocuses, lupine, forsythia, and fireflies hatched overnight, as they welcomed riots of dandelions. Some breezes were so feathery I stopped to savor them. As a rumpled stratosphere rocked with lightning and thunder, every thunderstorm was a ceremony.

My natal Eastern Woodlands evoked a lifetime on earth, during which children were born, became a family—our family—and left. Bonds that once seemed unseverable turned out not to be bonds at all.

By August, blueberries and huckleberries covered knolls and surrounded lakes. Early dusks and frigid rains alternated between sea fog and a flying moon mask.

A year later we stayed into fall and watched a medicinal parade: yellow-orange tansy along roadsides, blue and violet asters, milkweed spun to silk, black chokeberries on rocky summits.

In the aughts, I bonded with our Manset place, recovering Emily Dickinson's "sacrament of summer days." I had memorized the poem in high school. Now I knew that the "last communion in the haze" wasn't just the end of the baseball season; it was the destiny of every creature, rabbit or crow, when Great Winter arrives.

As I swam in Echo Lake, memories of worlds long dormant pealed through every cell. I experienced the essential riddle of life on earth— the magnificence of this vivid and various a vision, of strangers found and lost. I flipped onto my back in starfish mimesis, arms and legs extending and drawn back for propulsion, clouds blown to shreds above—in awe of what existence is, a Now of sky and mind.

In November 2011, rain-sleet downpour mostly rain, Lindy and I rose early for *chi gung* in Town Hill, a twelve-mile drive. Halfway there, we stopped behind a school bus, red lights flashing, children in rain gear led by mothers across 102.

Windshield wipers thrummed over droplets thickening into ice. Gusting leaves pasted onto wet stone. Shiny black road-top reflected houses and trees in impasto strokes like a Dutch masterpiece.

As we waited, I remembered carpooling for our son's kindergarten in Vermont. We had been delivered, as surely as by capsule, to time's nether side.

Snowfalls of virgin crystal came with December. We dug out cars and sent snapshots of snowmen to grandchildren.

We kept that house for eighteen years, the last six of which we lived in Maine full-time. Then, each of us struggling with late-onset inner darkness, we returned to California where our kids lived. I joked that they wanted us to die where it was convenient.

Two years later, we were back on Mount Desert. The summons west had been wrong, but like many wrong summonses, it pointed the way. Nothing in fabled Cali had proven to be what it seemed when we moved from Vermont to winter-less hippie paradise in our early thirties with two young children. We had left the stormish seasons of our respective Denver and New York upbringings to dwell in a Mediterranean clime and fashion a business and home for ourselves and our whelps. It worked until, like all magic and dreams, it dissolved into the spell from which it once arose. In the backdrop of gardener-tended yards and streets traversed by *E.T.: The Extraterrestrial,* a sense of "irie" and mall-world reigned. I didn't find my way out for thirty-eight years, the sense that *none of this is really real.*

After I walked the abyss, I became a participant again, at a more observant and grateful level, the "tender and callow fellow"* of a score I heard at nineteen and sought as a baffled pilgrim. The psychic zip file opened and told me secrets I never imagined learning in this lifetime, notes

---

*"Try to Remember" from *The Fantasticks,* lyrics and music by Tom Jones and Harvey Schmidt.

foreshadowed at an Amherst swimming hole and monk's sunrise.

I walked through Bar Harbor to the sand bar connecting village to isle. I watched it be covered and uncovered by tides, sea birds rising and falling on the anomaly. I scanned Mount Desert's synchronicity sinkhole for a new science and wrote this book. I had composed its forerunner, *Bottoming Out the Universe,* in the underworld.

In February, I played village pond hockey amid fallen branches, reeds, and icicles.

In the spring, I reconvened the Manset psychic group in Bar Harbor, first time since 2016. We were quick to protect Frenchman Bay from Norwegian salmon pens, as we projected tiaras of roses, floating candles, dragons, and flying lanterns. We received clairsentient calls for healing and sent reiki-like runes to friends, family, and strangers, present and in absentia, in this world and having crossed. We invited the weeping willow and crows to join our circle.

The following autumn, I hiked up Penobscot to Sargent peak with new friends Andrew and Sarah. We watched a wounded porcupine waddling in Dreamtime quills. We collected some of the season's last black chokeberries for my companions to extract antiviral tinctures. But we dallied long and ended up on a roundabout trail nearing dusk, three minor mountains yet to be crossed. At the third we climbed a facing of moraine for a third of a mile. I was panting, dripping sweat, as a lowing sun cut the horizon. We descended Parkman in a halo of purple gold. We left the forest just before the bears began to play.

"It was initiatory," Andrew remarked, as we parted at our cars.

We walk the lonesome valley without landmarks, without company, without promise. Of course, it's impossible; that's why we do it. If it were merely possible, it wouldn't be worth a whole universe. One look at a night of stars *tells you it is.*

EPILOGUE
Camouflage Cosmoses, Callings, and Codes

TECHNOCRACY

There is a fundamental difference between the astronomical sky, or outer space, and space in an ontological sense. Jeff Bezos and Elon Musk imagined colonizing the Solar System, but they did not understand the difference between actual and ideational sky. Gaia is the only place in the Solar System where life forms like us can breathe. Eager technocrats should remember. It is the lone world other than Mars where astronauts can land without instantly burning to a crisp or freezing solid.

Mars may have been inhabited once by intelligent "primates" who left a Sphinx-like face, pyramids, and glass viaducts, still discernible after 500,000 years of erosion. But what they breathed is gone.

Several moons of Jovian planets harbor rock- and glacier-covered oceans warmed by tidal shear in which rotifer-like, jellyfish-like, worm-like, fish-like, octopus-like, and/or dugong-like creatures might dwell, knowing ice as sky.

Phosphenes have been discovered in the atmosphere of Venus. Can fire salamanders breathe at 733 degrees Kelvin under ninety times Gaia's atmospheric pressure? What is the benchmark for life?

The few exo-planets we discern are mostly Jovian gasballs, too close to or far from stars that are too bright or too dim to incubate our sort of biosphere. Some of their eccentric orbits take them from Mercury-like forges to Neptune-like iceballs. At their metallic cores, diamonds fall as snow.

From a Dzogchen view, this life is altar and view, its meaning determined by where we locate ourselves and our relation to the software of access—the mirror, the TESS (Transiting Exoplanet Survey Satellite) data, and the curvature of the gross zone.

An old cowboy song captures the extraterrestrial quality of Sol 3 as mirrored by an imaginal wrangler on another planet. This is no bland cowpuncher ballad; it is a bottomless kōan:

> At midnight when the cattle are sleeping, / on my saddle I pillow my head, / and up at the heavens lie peeping, / from out of my cold grassy bed. / And it's often and often / I've wondered / at night while lying alone / if each tiny star way up yonder / is a great peopled world like our own. / In the evening in the bright stars up yonder / do cowboys lie down to their rest? / Do they gaze at this wide world and wonder / if roughriders dash o'er its crest? / Do they listen to the wolves in the canyon? / Do they watch the night owl in its flight? / Are their horses their only companions / while guarding their herds through the night?[1]

We are transported from "Home, Home on the Range" to an unsignified world among sun-stars, a landscape unaccountably the same as ours with its own "prairie lullaby." The Cosmic Witness in us is sighting Earth as a distant planet, its ranges populated by curious cowboys, its canyons resounding with howling wolves. They don't have to be humanoid "cowboys"; their "cattle" don't have to be cattle, the "wolves" don't have to be wolves. After all, similitude is a perfect disguise for the Other.

By *not* bringing extraterrestrial purviews into the foregrounds of their stories, writers like Fyodor Dostoevsky and William Faulkner disclose their presence everywhere. Could anything orbiting another star be stranger than Charles Dickens's Miss Havisham in her faded wedding dress, wedding cake rotting on the table, spiders running in and out, clocks stopped, candlelight fluttering on cobwebs? Not "alien invader" or "princess of Mars" strange, but strange as an existential event in an unsignified universe.[2]

It is possible that this Formation, not just the Solar System, Galaxy, and Laniakea Supercluster, of which the Milky Way and Andromeda are affiliates, but the whole ball of fire and wax, may be a condensation of a greater wave seeking expression, design, and experience, the thoughtform of a demiurge like Olaf Stapledon's 1937 *Star Maker.* At our densely downward station, drizzles and sleets are Physical-Etheric and most planets are uninhabitable, but the greater System is teeming with life and communications in sixth to twelfth (Astral through Monadic) dimensions, as is the multiverse in its myriad dimensionalities. What we experience now is a "camouflage cosmos," a crest of trans-dimensional depth effects.[3]

Despite its two trillion galaxies, Earth still sits at the center of the universe, the cosmos of Robert Fludd, Elias Ashmole, and their alchemical compatriots, a tourist destination for spirits and psychoids everywhere. Copernicus and Galileo solved a *different* riddle.

The notion that mankind can and should surpass nature has become the most deep-seated credo of modernity, even in eco circles. Green activists and conservationists promote nature-friendlier machines, sustainable technologies: Pelton wheels, solar battery storage, and System 001/B: floating filters and sensors to siphon plastic out of oceanic garbage gyres.

Songwriter Neil Young may have renounced genetically modified corn with his 2015 anti-biotech playlist, *The Monsanto Years,* but he valorized genetically modified transfers into cells and ribosomes with his Spotify kerfuffle in 2022.

Biomod isn't limited to soybeans, corn, and vaccines; it is a universal strategy that hacks codes and splices gene drives to exterminate polities and pests of no value to the oligarchy—*ex post facto* terraforming. Except that it is the opposite of making Mars, the Moon, or Jovian moons more earthlike. . . . It is techno-forming, making Earth itself less marshy and wooded, more amenable to corporate rule.

In a hypothetical future of CRISPR cuttings and computer-generated clones, medicine will be conducted by software entries, algorithms,

Zoom, and Amazon Prime. One dose of code comprising xenobots and other artificial animals will handle all micro- and nano-intruders, from comets, spores, or wet markets; it will disarm supergerms, mosquitos, and ticks, reprogram birth defects, erase unwanted traits, and fill needs and desires (or their surrogates) too. Robots aboard shopping malls launched by descendants of SpaceX, Virgin Galactic, and Blue Origin will handle medical deliveries from suborbital call centers. If all goes well . . .

Technocracy wants—needs, presumes—to take over infinity, as dowry and prerogative. It has a warrant: Without increasingly higher tech, we can't escape an economic collapse and major die-off or recover our massive down-payment in hardware, infrastructure, supply chains, and belief systems. The conviction that technology is the only way and, if not perfect, as perfect as things will ever get, is the ultimate rabbit hole *because it doesn't look like a rabbit hole.*

The same mindset has replaced life with a *game called life,* and without Buddhist players to mediate Hindu gods. Everyone is touting their own God brand in an attempt to stay on a scientist-as-magician, commodity-as-destiny course. The mindset proposes to solve the climate, energy, and health crises by dumping light-reflecting metals in the atmosphere, painting buildings white, sterilizing mosquitos, and implanting computers and neurolinks in everything that moves. It is near impossible to conceive of a future Earth, short of a superstorm-ridden "Waterworld" or super-germ locked-down favela, that is not ruled by a global elite of technocrats. Beyond a few remaining Amazon tribes, neo-survivalists, and sasquatches, this paradigm is as ineluctable as it is hegemonous.[4]

The Elon Musk/Bill Gates/Jeff Bezos hell-realm may be a fantasy, but most people await and welcome it. If God gets killed in the process—well, she can be resurrected as a programming archangel in a new Godworld.

Techgnosis is not wrong: once nature and culture got entangled, it was all nature (molecule, algorithm, biont) and all culture (symbol, sign, society). The rusting cyberware among dandelions and asters bred the fungus digesting trash. Cyber-anthropologist Terrence Deacon provides an elegant diptych: "Physically we're just another ape, mentally we're a whole new phylum of organisms."[5]

The original Stone Age dream was a projection of power over the unknown. Once civilization has tamed and re-engineered the planet's geological, biological, and meteorological affairs and terraformed the Solar System, humanity will be safe at last, king of matter and energy. Society won't have to deal with wayward winds, viral variants, or wolf packs, or be at risk of Gaian blowback. Turn on the faucet, water comes. Flip the switch, space is lit. Click on Zoom, a person across the planet appears.

Civilization's addiction to a vending-machine bliss realm and depleted phenomenology is the current global driver: a blend of necropolitics and techno-futurism. Folks want to feed and be fed by the beast because they want the beast to be real. My Facebook friend Darin De Stefano exposed the bogus miracle whip:

> Transhumanism is nothing but subhumanism on advertising steroids. And what it is selling is a kind of omnicidal dehumanization that is explicitly anti-biological. One cannot exceed a humanity which has been boldly counterfeited into nonexistence. We would have to have become human first, a task at which we've staggeringly failed. . . .
>
> Adding dead things to yourself or yourself to dead things doesn't "exceed your humanity." It renders it ironic. The result isn't a "superman." It's a living being so confused that it replaced parts of itself with doll-parts and machines and shit.[6]

Whether COVID-19 is a gain-of-function escapee from a lab or a zoonotic mutation, the masses receive it on the fear channel, which is as fierce, frightened, and fallback as the terror of being stalked on a trail by a bear or bobcat. All other contingencies, leeways, wildlife-corridor and greenbelt vows are dropped. That's the way it's been, from Pliocene vulpines to delta and omicron spikes. French philosopher and Algerian war vet Paul Virilio said, "Interactivity keeps the world in a kind of tetanic trance, at once inert and overexcited, sleepwalking on a planetary scale."[7] The fear channel is the Satanic rebuttal to God.

THE GOD CODE

Forbidden archaeology proposes a Tartaria-like advanced civilization during the 24.6-million-year-long Silurian epoch, which has been corroded to kibbles or gamed. We can't remember or excavate relics of Atlantis and Lemuria, so we are at risk of repeating them. Ancestral atavism means rapt worship of machines and potions—robots fashioned of bits and gears, life forms scanned by black magic, alembics and athanors in the markets of the Empire.

Pre-Pleistocene wheels, sprockets, discs, clocks, orreries, rings, runes, diodes, and glyphs tell us that Atlantis *was real*. The missing continent stands for an earlier conflation of technology and magic whereby a whole civilization was possessed and destroyed by its 'bots, potions, interfaces, and wraiths. Those who search for a sunken continent in the Atlantic overly objectify a myth, but those who consider Atlantis only an epoch on another plane without terrestrial coordinates spiritually bypass the sub-astral, quasi-etheric geosphere.[8]

In the "starseed calling" of Azores-based psychic Patricia Cori, archetypal geometric forms, imbedded astrally and etherically in our DNA, repair and rebuild not only damaged life codons but God codes—links to the Divine Energy Field of All That Is. By a transposition of DNA's permanent seed, recapitulated and brewed in bogs and hot springs of matter, individuals can slip the loop of artificial intelligence and mind control and proceed on the "ascension ladder" toward other states of existence and soul awakening.

Cori sees biotechnologies as damaging or wiping three key elements of our twelve-stranded signatures: (1) focused 7.83 Hz Schumann Resonance attunement—Extremely Low Frequency (ELF) waves in the Earth's magnetic field that interlock with our brainwaves and attune us to the beat of the planet; (2) fifth-dimensional ascension kits that allow us to make touch with guides and mages in deeper dimensions; (3) built-in Solfeggio frequencies, a six-tone scale that lets us chant and transmit sacred songs and songlines, blocking the zombie E.T.'s—or whoever they are—from dragging Earth into the Eighth Sphere of Illusion and occupying our reality. Losing these links, warns Cori, leads to soul loss: "to the disconnect of the God Code or Chip within us, the robotization of our species, the creation of soulless chimeras of their design, and the enslavement of sovereign souls."[9]

Deep in the ear canals of every living entity is an heirloom crystal that retains spirit's attunement to higher knowledge, lucid dreams, out-of-body journeyings, and transmissions from plants, animals, tinctures, and telepathies. During crises of near death, they become portals to the actual universe. The same crystalline substance tunes DNA to etheric, astral, and higher-plane portals, allowing spirits throughout All That Is to incarnate in matter.

In a Zoroastrian morality play, Luciferian and Ahrimanic forces are trying to destroy our planet while leading an evolution away from the God Code and transcendent consciousness toward the Mephistophelian Eighth Sphere. This hearkens back to a Manichean heresy: The earth realm is created by the fall of spirit into matter. Matter is still imbued with spirit, but its sacred aspect has been contaminated by a profane entity recruiting it into an untenanted plane of being.

The God Code permeates Eurasian religions from the Christ Consciousness of apostolic Apocrypha to Kether of the Hebrew Zohar to Brahma of the Hindu Vedas. As we look backward through a sword of phenomenological light that keeps us out of Eden, we harbor a spark of divine fire that transforms the mundane *Prakriti* (prime material energy) of Ignorance into a Vedantic *Prakriti* of Knowledge. The final signal or sephira, Malkhut (Kingship), remained partially intact, exiled in Shekhinah—divine feminine immanence—as spirit sank onto the material plane.

The Eighth Sphere is the great deception, the great illusion, the great seduction. It makes it look like the end of the end here, but it isn't; it's a hex, an induced apocalypse—a thoughtform that's taken hold, a conspiracy theory that's so persuasive, when you're inside it, it feels as though nothing else is real.

Anything that seems the least bit visionary or heartful is rejected because everybody knows *this* is it and we're *really* in for it now.

That gloom-and-doom hallucination is falling away. It was a conspiracy against Earth, against the power and vitality of what our existence and sacred planet *really are,* not the existence that science and technocracy tell us alone is real, which is devoid of soul.[10]

In the 2018–2021 NBC/Netflix series *Manifest,* fictional Flight 828 of Montego Air took off from Jamaica on April 7, 2013, passed through severe turbulence, and emerged on November 4, 2018, landing in New York. Its passengers, after debarking, tried to reclaim their lives and loved ones. Only hours had passed for them, but everyone else had traveled five-and-a-half years. Many experienced "callings," sudden entheogen-like breaks in reality, often with occult or mythological imagery—peacocks, angels, Egyptian hieroglyphs—as well as lucid returns to alternate, catastrophic versions of flight 828, with more extreme turbulence followed by crash scenes. In revisitations of the flight as well as other callings, they were enveloped in clouds, smoke, lightning, storms, blood, and supernatural phenomena during which their own voice or that of a fellow passenger prompted them to carry out some assignment without telling them what or how. The callings were collective riddles around their altered DNA, woven together like clues in a Gaia-scale geocaching.

The series developed a cult following for a reason—"callings" are a bellwether of our time. We have all passed through a 2020 gateway, a psychic wormhole and vibration-shift, and are being asked to find new coordinates and meanings. At a crossroads of cargo cults and conspiracy theories, coincidences and clues speak for alt-Earth. Callings replace facts; people make up stories, even if they don't believe them, because they sense the power of divination. Those QAnon acolytes who gathered in Dallas's Dealey Plaza weren't wrong, they were a thousand years early, as they arranged themselves in a giant Q.

The turbulence encountered by Montego Air was archetypally the "tempest" or transhistorical storm overtaking Shakespeare's vessel bearing King Alonso of Naples with his entourage, its shipwreck modelled on the 1609 loss of the *Sea Venture* off Bermuda, foreshadowing the Bermuda triangle, which mysteriously swallowed ships, planes, and people. *Forbidden Planet* indeed!* Two vessels (and a starship) land in

---

*I am referencing a 1956 movie about a twenty-third-century starship, an adaptation of Shakespeare's *Tempest.*

magic, time-altered lands, and a magician's daughter speaks for each as she cries, *"If by your art, my dearest father, you have / Put the wild waters in this roar, allay them."*[11]

Ours is a full flight: seven billion plus, moving at more than a thousand miles per hour with other planets, solar systems, and galaxies.

Oh, brave new world, allay!

BANDWIDTHS

In October 2021, an old friend and author of mine, science buff Richard Hoagland, invited me on his podcast, *The Other Side of Midnight*, to discuss the role of animals—actual mice, birds, dogs, cats, as well as poltergeist ones and borderline cryptids that could have been either creatures or spirits (or both)—as messengers between the world of spirit and the world of matter. An esoteric seeker usually tethered to evidence-based etiquettes, Richard had extended his domain to allow messages from folks who had crossed from this incarnation to an afterworld. His late-in-life partner, homeopathic doctor Robin Falkov, had died prematurely two and a half years earlier and, since then, mice in his house had been setting scraps of paper, dust, and other debris in configurations representing Cydonia and other aspects of his Martian and hyperdimensional modeling. After reminding me that his extraterrestrial pyramids mirrored and reverse-mirrored actual Egyptian pyramids, Richard concluded:

> That [mirroring] records, by whatever civilization was on Mars at the time, a transition between a state of existence where we were in another dimension, and then we flipped; we were—shall we say, mirror-reversed—to where we are now in an artificial prison . . . and what we are experiencing . . . is a deliberate *artificial* dimensional separation from the higher dimensionality that we used to occupy and freely migrate between. And this set of monuments on Mars is designed to tell us there was this sudden transition, and because of the proper motion of the Belt stars of Orion, I can actually put a date when that might have occurred.
>
> Okay. That's a model—that we are basically in a phantom zone.

. . . A few weeks ago, a brilliant young astrophysicist published a paper to the effect that Earth may be trapped inside a giant magnetic tunnel. If there has been a dimensional shift but there is some kind of interface with three-dimensional reality as we know it, there should be some kind of signature, some kind of electromagnetic noise or signal or boundary condition which would give it away.

This astrophysicist shows with a diagram that in this section of the Milky Way about 350 light years out and extending in lateral directions along the spiral arm, there is this weird tunnel or tube of magnetic flux and particle radiation *etcetera etcetera,* almost like it's the interface between a higher dimensional shift and our lower three-dimensional—quote—reality. And the most significant part is that the tunnel, this measurable-now-with-physics constraint of electromagnetism is between us and the Belt stars of Orion, meaning that we could literally be seeing the universe as a mirror image in the larger Galaxy from where we think we're seeing inside this artificially created bubble. And that would explain why it's so damn difficult for Robin to communicate across the boundary—because the bandwidth is so incredibly restricted, and it can only operate at certain periods of time conforming to what I term a "hyperdimensional astrological configuration of appropriate geometry" in the Solar System that makes intermittent communication even possible at all. . . .

Robin literally died at the first moment that the sun was coming over the horizon here in New Mexico . . . and that's when the physics goes boing! So a conduit opens at dawn. That's why prisoners are executed at dawn. That's why raiding parties go out at dawn. The whole thing has to do with that connection momentarily as the sun peeks over the horizon as we're rotating toward it.[12]

Hoagland's oft-misunderstood vision sees through many glasses darkly. It starts with NASA-photographed artifacts on Sol 4 and proceeds through transdimensional geometry and cosmic conspiracies to the gateway of dark matter and dark knowledge. It is as if we exist at the surface of our own dimensional depth while the paradigm (or bubble) that holds us is dissolving, and a greater sun is rising from the dark ages of camouflage civilization to reveal an amphitheater in which a gladiatorial sideshow has been taking place.

New mimeses have been forming, coalescing, occulting, reemerging. Dreamings billow and wither in the various winds, as the filigree of each reality flutters against the veil of *all* realities. At grand centrals, world lines cross and we see the unseen, hear the unheard, feel a hand or wing or antennae through the veil.

Butterflies appear in Broadway theaters. There is barking but no dog, cawing but no crow, footsteps but no feet. The smell of a deceased person's cologne spreads without molecules. A ghost cat mews. Yes, Hamlet, there are "more things on heaven and earth than are dreamt of in our philosophy."[13]

Spirits are pinging electronic devices, tapping into Zoom chats, dispatching thoughtforms in the clairsentient range of ravens and cats. The comatose in hospitals are phoning home, miraculously cured, to say goodbye *while never waking from their comas.*

The disconnect is not because they are speaking too softly—they are neither soft nor loud—it is because our attention is entrained or entranced. In fact, they are screaming, flooding us with information, while we are engrossed in clatter and internal noise.

Clairsentience, like the poet's fog, *"sits looking / over harbor and city / on silent haunches / and then moves on."*[14]

The key to unidentified flying—or mermaiding, salamandering, leprechauning, saucering—guides is *information,* changing form as it crosses platforms. Its peeps and pokes herald a reunion of spirit and matter, the living and the dead, in one land: *our* land.

For Janus's days alee, I close my book with occult astronomer Rodney Collin's augury:

"When a new gift, a new possibility, is given to the earth, it is always presented in two ways—in unconscious form and in conscious form. In the hydrogen bomb we recognize the unconscious form of a power heretofore unknown on earth. We await the demonstration of the same power in conscious form, that is, incarnate in living beings."[15]

That we do.

Notes

PREFACE. READING GATEWAY CARDS

1. I rewrote my definitions of alchemy and astrology from the chapter "Chaos Magic" in *The Return of the Tower of Babel*.
2. Loeb, *Extraterrestrial*, 25–46, 191.
3. Laura Matsue, Facebook post, August 5, 2020.

CHAPTER ONE. PLANET

1. Ploum, "Zon en Zonnebloem," in *Spiegel van het Universum*, 26–27.
2. Swimme, *The Universe Story: From the Primordial Flaring Forth to the Ecozoic Era—A Celebration of the Unfolding of the Cosmos.* See also Swimme, *The Hidden Heart of the Cosmos*, 112.
3. Forere Motioheloa and Paul Simon, "Boy in the Bubble," *Graceland*, Warner Brothers, 1987.
4. Hesiod, *Theogony*, translated by Hugh G. Evelyn-White, modified by Barry F. Vaughan.
5. For the formation of Earth and its landscapes, I rewrote sections from *Embryogenesis: Species, Gender, and Identity*, particularly the chapters "The Original Earth," "The Materials of Life," "The First Beings," "The Cell," and "Sperm and Egg," 13–132.
6. Steiner, *Cosmic Memory: Atlantis and Lemuria.* See also the chapter "Spiritual Embryogenesis" in Grossinger, *Embryogenesis*, 694–724, and Grossinger, *Dark Pool of Light, Volume 2: Consciousness in Psychospiritual and Psychic Ranges*, 84.

7. Steiner, "The Hyperoborean and the Polarian Epochs" in *Cosmic Memory: Atlantis and Lemuria.*

8. Strieber, *The Afterlife Revolution,* 160–62, 165.

9. Strieber, *The Afterlife Revolution,* 163.

10. Khenchen Palden Sherab Rinpoche and Khenpo Tsewang Dongyal Rinpoche, *Splendid Presence of the Great Guhyagarbha,* 8.

11. My summary of the Anthropocene is based, in part, on Stephanie Wakefield, *Anthropocene Back Loop: Experimentation in Unsafe Operating Space (Critical Climate Chaos: Irreversibility).* See my review of this book on Amazon.com and on my website, www.richard grossinger.com.

12. Inner Traditions publisher Ehud Sperling told me this story about his time among Australian Aborigines while helping to develop Robert Lawlor's *Voices of the First Day.*

13. Peirce, *Collected Papers,* vol. 1, paragraph 284.

14. Roth, "His Holiness the Sixteenth Karmapa at Hopi Mesa," kagyu.org, 1974.

CHAPTER TWO. GENOME

1. Delbert, "Crows Are Self-Aware and 'Know What They Know,' Just Like Humans," *Yahoo Life,* January 9, 2021.

2. Grossinger, *Bottoming Out the Universe,* 95.

3. Margulis and Sagan, *Origins of Sex,* 63, 169.

4. Lynn Margulis, personal communication, February 21, 1999.

5. Grossinger, *Embryogenesis,* "Sperm and Egg," 109–32.

6. Grossinger, *Embryogenesis,* "Self and Desire," 677–94.

7. Grossinger, *Embryogenesis,* 579.

8. Margulis and Sagan, 206.

9. For a slightly different version of this concept, see Grossinger, *Bottoming Out the Universe,* 97 *et seq.*

10. I adapted this line from Charles Olson's remark about Paris of Greece and Helen of Troy during the 1965 Berkeley Poetry Conference.

11. Karlsen, *The Terrain Is Everything: An Ontology of Inter-species Becoming,* unpublished manuscript.

12. De Stefano, personal communication, January 17, 2021.

13. Fasano and Flaherty, *Gut Feelings: The Microbiome and Our Health.*

14. Bush, "Zack Bush on COVID-19, Glyphosate, and the Nature of Viruses,"

LiveHealthyBeWell, Stitcher.com, June 23, 2020. The section integrates Bush's explanation with my own speculations.

CHAPTER THREE. DREAMINGS

1. The account of butterflies in Copenhagen is rewritten from *2018 Europe Trip Journal* on my website, www.richardgrossinger.com. The colors blue and yellow were taken from *Bardo of Waking Life,* 87.
2. Swain, *A Place for Strangers: Toward a History of Australian Aborigine Being,* 21.
3. Friedlander, discussed in Grossinger, *Dark Pool of Light, Volume 2: Consciousness in Psychospiritual and Psychic Ranges,* 218–19. The original source of this material through Note 10 was a series of Friedlander tele-classes and class notes in 2010. One class was titled "Etheric Energy and Magic."
4. Borax and Lonsdale, *Cosmic Weather Report,* 187.
5. Friedlander, discussed in Grossinger, *Dark Pool of Light, Volume 2: Consciousness in Psychospiritual and Psychic Ranges,* 220.
6. Friedlander, discussed in Grossinger, *Dark Pool of Light, Volume 2: Consciousness in Psychospiritual and Psychic Ranges,* 221.
7. Friedlander, discussed in Grossinger, *Dark Pool of Light, Volume 2: Consciousness in Psychospiritual and Psychic Ranges,* 223–24.
8. Friedlander, discussed in Grossinger, *Dark Pool of Light, Volume 2: Consciousness in Psychospiritual and Psychic Ranges,* 229–30.
9. Friedlander, discussed in Grossinger, *Dark Pool of Light, Volume 2: Consciousness in Psychospiritual and Psychic Ranges,* 228–30.
10. Friedlander, discussed in Grossinger, *Dark Pool of Light, Volume 2: Consciousness in Psychospiritual and Psychic Ranges,* 233.
11. Lawlor, *Voices of the First Day,* 45–48.
12. Swain, *A Place for Strangers: Toward a History of Australian Aborigine Being,* 21.
13. Dean, "Octopus and Squid Evolution Is Officially Weirder Than We Could Have Ever Imagined," *Science Alert,* March 6, 2019.
14. Anomolian.com, "Octopus DNA Is Not of This World, Numerous Researchers Conclude," August 22, 2021.
15. *My Octopus Teacher,* directed by Pippa Ehrlich and James Reed, Netflix, 2020.
16. Dodé Kalpa Zangpo, quoted in Sogyal Rinpoche, *Dzogchen and Padmasambhava,* 83.

17. Sturtevant, *Handbook of North American Indians: Southwest.*

18. Lévi-Strauss, *The Raw and the Cooked.*

19. I have combined multiple internet descriptions of tardigrades. See also Spector, "Frozen tardigrade becomes first 'quantum entangled' animal in history, researchers claim," LiveScience.com, December 20, 2021.

20. The description of pigeons awaking in Siena is adapted from my *2006 Europe Trip Journal* on my website, www.richardgrossinger.com.

21. Ross Hamilton, email, Cincinnati, Ohio, August 17, 2021.

22. Matthew Wood, email, Martell, Wisconsin, January 12, 2021.

23. George Mattingly, Facebook post, September 5, 2021.

CHAPTER FOUR. META-SCIENCES

1. Sam M. Lewis, "For All We Know," 1934.

2. Peake, *Is There Life After Death,* 40.

3. Peake, *Is There Life After Death,* 45.

4. I am grateful to Keith Thompson for crystallizing this concept. I am presently helping oversee his makeover of his classic 1990s book *Angels and Aliens: UFOs and the Mythic Imagination* into a 2023 magnum opus, *Cosmos Calling: UFOs and the Human Response* under the Sacred Planet Books imprint I am curating for Inner Traditions.

5. For Nassim Haramein's ideas, see www.resonancescience.org.

6. Tsoknyi Rinpoche, *Fearless Simplicity,* pp. 46–47.

7. Cocteau, *Orphée,* script-o-rama.com.

CHAPTER FIVE. UNIDENTIFIED GUIDES

1. James Fox (director), *The Phenomenon,* 2020.

2. McFall, "Rubio Wants Answers on 'UFOs' Reported over US Military Posts," Fox News Online, May 23, 2021.

3. Lewis-Kraus, "How the Pentagon Started Taking UFOs Seriously," *New Yorker,* May 10, 2021.

4. McFall, "Rubio Wants Answers on 'UFOs' Reported over US Military Posts," Fox News Online, May 23, 2021.

5. Hynek, *The UFO Experience: A Scientific Inquiry.*

6. Grossinger, *The Night Sky,* 721–22.

7. Grossinger, *Martian Homecoming at the All-American Revival Church,* 89.

8. Grossinger, *The Night Sky*, 721.

9. Jim Jacobs and Warren Casey, "Summer Nights" from the musical *Grease*, RSO, 1978.

10. Davis, *TechGnosis*, 119, 364–65.

11. Lindell, interviews with Harold Augspurger, Commander 415th Night Fighter Squadron; Frederic Ringwald, S-2 Intelligence Officer, 415th Night Fighter Squadron in "A Historical and Physiological Perspective of the Foo Fighters of World War Two."

12. Grossinger, *Bottoming Out the Universe*, 253.

13. For the information in the preceding paragraphs, see Petr Vachler, *Top Secret UFO Projects: Declassified*, Netflix, 2021.

14. Schwab, *Cutting Remarks*, back cover. This trope is much more fully developed in the "Saturnalia" chapter of *The Return of the Tower of Babel* where it is integrated with Stephen, Proctor, "Trump Supporter at CPAC Rails against Election Fraud Lies: 'Show Me the Freakin' Kraken,'" Yahoo Entertainment, July 13, 2021, and a discussion of the "Stop the Steal" egregore leading to the January 6, 2021 "Saturnalia."

15. The account of David Wilcock at Noniland is adapted from "Kaua'i 2010 Trip" under "Travel Journals" on my website, www.richardgrossinger.com.

16. The section on psychoids is reconstructed from *Dark Pool of Light, Volume 3 The Crisis and Future of Consciousness*, 193–95.

17. Jung, "The Tavistock Lectures: On the Theory and Practice of Analytical Psychology," in *The Symbolic Life: Miscellaneous Writings, The Collected Works of C. G. Jung*, vol. 18, 765–68. This section of my discussion on Jung and psychoids is rewritten from Grossinger, *The Night Sky: Soul and Cosmos*, 543–51.

CHAPTER SIX. INCARNATIONS

1. Shakespeare, *Macbeth*, Act 5, Scene 5, lines 24–26.

2. Taylor and Winquist, *Encyclopedia of Postmodernism*, 113.

3. McKenna, "Dreaming Awake at the End of Time."

4. Plato, *The Apology of Socrates*, translated by Benjamin Jowett.

5. Barrington, *JOTT: when things disappear . . . and come back or relocate—and why it really happens*.

6. Lonsdale, personal communications, 1991, 2020, and 2021 combined.

7. Bob Simmons, email, September 10, 2021.

8. McKay, *The Luminous Landscape of the Afterlife: Jordan's Message to the Living on What to Expect After Death*, 87–88.

9. McKay, *The Luminous Landscape of the Afterlife*, pp. xii–xiii. As an editor of this book, I helped Matt frame his relation to Jordan in the preface. I am borrowing my own edit back here.

10. See Grossinger, *Bottoming Out the Universe*, 133.

11. Moaveni, *Guest House for Young Widows*, 127.

12. The description of the World Trade Center is adapted from *2013: Raising the Earth to the Next Vibration*, 192–93.

13. Friedlander, *Recentering Seth*, 335. I put this book together by transcribing material from John's classes, occasionally editing in things he said to me personally.

14. Cocteau, *Orphée*, script-o-rama.com.

15. New Testament, John 11:25–26.

16. "Screenplays for You," https://sfy.ru/.

17. This section is adapted from *The Night Sky*, 318.

18. Dorn, *Slinger*, unpaginated (three pages from the end).

19. McKenna, "The Last Interview, A Conversation with Erik Davis," Big Island, Hawaii, Soundcloud, November 1999.

20. McKenna, "Dreaming Awake at the End of Time," a lecture recorded by Sound Photosynthesis, San Francisco, December 13, 1998.

21. Friedlander, *Recentering Seth*, 49–50.

22. Strieber, *The Afterlife Revolution*, 120.

23. Strieber, *The Afterlife Revolution*, 10.

24. Shakespeare, *The Tempest*, Act 5, Scene 1, lines 217–18.

25. Wilder, *The Bridge of San Luis Rey*, 235.

26. See my account in Grossinger, *Bottoming Out the Universe*, 52–80.

27. Kean, *Surviving Death*, 61.

28. Kean, *Surviving Death*, 78.

29. See my account in Grossinger, *Bottoming Out the Universe*, 103–11.

30. Wendell Seavey, personal communication, January 2020.

31. There are many different versions of this tale. I fashioned my own.

CHAPTER SEVEN. PRACTICES

I wrote the "Initiation" section of this chapter while I was also working on two presently unpublished memoir-like novels, *Out of Babylon* and *Episodes in Disguise of a Marriage*. The narrative here is adapted from their narratives.

1. Weinberg, *The First Three Minutes,* 154.
2. Overbye, review of Brian Greene, *Until the End of Time: Mind, Matter, and Our Search for Meaning in an Evolving Universe, New York Review of Books,* March 8, 2020, 15.
3. Grossinger, *Bottoming Out the Universe,* 2.
4. Grossinger, *Bottoming Out the Universe,* 224–25.
5. Yale college "Whiffenpoof Song."
6. This paragraph and other indirect Dzogchen references in my discussions of Buddhism in this chapter were gleaned from Khenpo Tsewang Dongyal Rinpoche, Winter Dzogchen Retreat, Palm Beach Dharma Center, Jupiter, Florida (made available live on Vimeo), January 2022.
7. Grossinger, *Bottoming Out the Universe,* 159.
8. Grossinger, *Dark Pool of Light, Volume 2: Consciousness in Psychospiritual and Psychic Ranges,* 105–6.
9. Grossinger, *Bottoming Out the Universe,* 274.
10. Grossinger, *2013: Raising the Earth to the Next Vibration,* 112.
11. I developed this argument out of *Dark Pool of Light, Volume 2: Consciousness in Psychospiritual and Psychic Ranges,* 298–301.
12. Charles Stein, Facebook post from earlier journal notes, August 2021.
13. Friedlander, *Recentering Seth,* 68.
14. Charles Stein, Facebook post from earlier journal notes, August 2021. With his permission, I have repunctuated and rearranged my friend's entry.
15. Ron Sieh, email, July 11, 2021.
16. Kyger, untitled poem in Grossinger (ed.), *Ecology and Consciousness,* 3.
17. Williams, "Asphodel, That Greeny Flower" in *Journey to Love.*
18. Blake, "The Marriage of Heaven and Hell," written 1793, *The Portable Blake,* 250.
19. Singer, *The Untethered Soul,* 100, 103–6.
20. Wheelwright, ed. *The Presocratics,* 73.
21. Whitney, *Map of the Heart: An East-West Understanding of Heart Intelligence,* unpublished manuscript.
22. Whitney, *Map of the Heart: An East-West Understanding of Heart Intelligence,* unpublished manuscript.
23. Chödrön, *The Places That Scare You: A Guide to Fearlessness in Difficult Times,* 128.
24. Grossinger, *New Moon: A Coming-of-Age Tale,* 502.
25. Friedlander, *Recentering Seth,* 351–52.

EPILOGUE. CAMOUFLAGE COSMOSES, CALLINGS, AND CODES

1. "Cowboy's Meditation," published in N. Howard Thorp, *Songs of the Cowboy* (self-published pamphlet, 1908). This book was edited and republished by Alice Corbin Henderson, assistant editor of *Poetry* magazine (Boston and New York: Houghton Mifflin Company, 1921). She writes, "I regret that I do not know the author's name. Have tried to locate him, but so far have failed. Heard this sung in Bluff City, Utah, by an old puncher named Carter." The book was republished by cowboy balladeer Don Edwards (Weatherford, Texas: Singin' Hills Cattle Co./Sevenshoux Publishing, 1991), as he adapted many of the lyrics and wanted to make them available to fans. The version I am quoting is Edwards's adaptation of the original. A version is also available in a John A. Lomax anthology in the digital commons. See the bibliography, under Lomax.
2. Adapted from Grossinger, *The Night Sky,* 616–17.
3. Roberts, *The Unknown Reality,* vol. 2, 344–47.
4. The "technocracy" section was grafted out of *The Return of the Tower of Babel,* particularly the sections entitled "The Future of the Genome" and "The Vaccine Is Not the Problem with the Vaccine."
5. Deacon, *The Symbolic Species,* 23.
6. Darin De Stefano, Facebook post, June 3, 2021.
7. Paul Virilio, quoted in Hickman, "Paul Virilio: The Anti-City," onscene .weebly.com, September 9, 2017.
8. The "Atlantis" section was grafted out of *The Return of the Tower of Babel,* particularly the section entitled "The Vaccine Is Not the Problem with the Vaccine."
9. Psychic medium Patricia Cori discusses this in her various Starseed books, including a forthcoming title, tentatively called *Hacking the God Cod.* Cori lives on the peaks of volcanic Atlantis, East Greenland time.
10. Ellias Lonsdale conveyed something like this, which I transformed in assimilating.
11. Shakespeare, *The Tempest,* Act 1, Scene 2, lines 1–2.
12. Hoagland, "The Consciousness of Crows . . . And Other Curious Creatures," *The Other Side of Midnight,* October 24, 2021.
13. Shakespeare, *Hamlet,* Act 1, Scene 5, lines 166–67.
14. Sandburg, "Fog," in *Chicago Poems,* 1916.
15. Collin, *The Theory of Conscious Harmony,* 191.

Bibliography

Anomalien.com. "Octopus DNA Is Not of This World, Numerous Researchers Conclude." August 22, 2021.

Barrington, Mary Rose. *JOTT: when things disappear . . . and come back or relocate—and why it really happens.* Charlottesville, VA: Anomalist Books, 2018.

Blake, William. *The Portable Blake.* Edited by Alfred Kazin. New York: Viking Press, 1946.

Borax, Mark, and Ellias Lonsdale. *Cosmic Weather Report: Notes from the Edge of the Universe.* Berkeley: North Atlantic Books, 2010.

Bush, Zack. "Zack Bush on COVID-19, Glyphosate, and the Nature of Viruses." *LiveHealthyBeWell.* Accessed at Stitcher.com, 2020.

Castaneda, Carlos. *The Teachings of Don Juan: A Yaqui Way of Knowledge.* Berkeley: University of California Press, 1969.

Chatwin, Bruce. *The Songlines.* New York: Penguin Books, 2012, originally published in 1987.

Chödrön, Pema. *The Places That Scare You: A Guide to Fearlessness in Difficult Times.* Boulder, Colo.: Shambhala Publications, 2018.

Cocteau, Jean, dir. *Orphée.* Paris, France: DisCina, 1950.

Collin, Rodney. *The Theory of Conscious Harmony.* London: Robinson and Watkins Books, 1958.

Cori, Patricia. *Hacking the God Code: The Conspiracy to Steal the Human Soul—How to Preserve, Protect, and Enhance Your DNA as You Ascend Out of the Matrix.* Rochester, Vt.: Inner Traditions, 2022.

Davis, Erik. *TechGnosis: Myth, Magic & Mysticism in the Age of Information.* Berkeley: North Atlantic Books, 2015.

Deacon, Terrence. *The Symbolic Species: The Co-evolution of Language and the Brain*. New York: W. W. Norton & Company, 1997.

Delbert, Catherine. "Crows Are Self-Aware and 'Know What They Know,' Just Like Humans." *Yahoo Life,* January 9, 2021.

Dean, Signe. "Octopus and Squid Evolution Is Officially Weirder Than We Could Have Ever Imagined." *Science Alert,* March 6, 2019.

Dorn, Edward. *Slinger*. Berkeley: Wingbow Press, 1975.

Ehrlich, Pippa, and James Reed, dirs. *My Octopus Teacher*. Netflix, 2020.

Eisenbud, Jule. "Interview." In *Ecology and Consciousness: Traditional Wisdom on the Environment*, edited by Richard Grossinger. Berkeley: North Atlantic Books, 1978.

Fasano, Alessio, and Susan Flaherty. *Gut Feelings: The Microbiome and Our Health*. Cambridge, Mass.: The MIT Press, 2021.

Fox, James, dir.. *The Phenomenon*. New York: 1091 Pictures, 2020.

Friedlander, John. *Recentering Seth: Teachings from a Multidimensional Entity on Living Gracefully and Skillfully in a World You Create But Do Not Control*. Rochester, Vt.: Bear & Company, 2022.

Grossinger, Richard. *2013: Raising the Earth to the Next Vibration*. Berkeley: North Atlantic Books, 2010.

———. *Bardo of Waking Life*. Berkeley: North Atlantic Books, 2008.

———. *Bottoming Out the Universe: Why There Is Something Rather Than Nothing*. Rochester, Vt.: Park Street Press, 2020.

———. *Dark Pool of Light, Volume 2: Consciousness in Psychospiritual and Psychic Ranges*. Berkeley, Calif.: North Atlantic Books, 2012.

———. *Dark Pool of Light, Volume 3: The Crisis and Future of Consciousness*. Berkeley, Calif.: North Atlantic Books, 2012.

———. *Ecology and Consciousness: Traditional Wisdom on the Environment*, edited by Richard Grossinger. Berkeley: North Atlantic Books, 1978.

———. *Embryogenesis: Species, Gender, and Identity*. Berkeley: North Atlantic Books, 2000.

———. *Martian Homecoming at the All-American Revival Church*. Plainfield, Vt.: North Atlantic Books, 1974.

———. *New Moon: A Coming-of-Age Tale*. Berkeley: North Atlantic Books, 2016.

———. *The Night Sky: Soul and Cosmos*. Berkeley: North Atlantic Books, 2014.

———. *The Return of the Tower of Babel: QAnon, COVID-19, and Chaos Magic,* title tentative, unpublished manuscript.

Herzog, Werner, dir. *Nomad: In the Footsteps of Bruce Chatwin*. London: Sideways Film, 2020.

Hesiod. *Theogony*. Translated by Hugh G. Evelyn-White (1914), modified by Barry F. Vaughan, barryfvaughan.org.

Hickman, Steven Craig. "Paul Virilio: The Anti-City." onscene.weebly.com, 2017.

Hynek, J. Allen. *The UFO Experience: A Scientific Inquiry*. New York: Ballantine Books, 1972.

Ibrahim, Samantha. "Woman Claims She's Married to Michael Jackson's Ghost: 'He Stays Possessed in Me," *New York Post,* August 17, 2021.

Jowett, Benjamin. *The Dialogues of Plato*. Oxford: Oxford University Press, 1892.

Jung, Carl. "The Tavistock Lectures: On the Theory and Practice of Analytical Psychology." In *The Symbolic Life: Miscellaneous Writings. The Collected Works of C. G. Jung*, vol 18. Edited by Gerhard Adler and R. F. C. Hull. Princeton, N.J.: Princeton University Press, 1968.

Jung, Carl G., and Wolfgang Pauli. *Atom and Archetype: The Pauli-Jung Letters, 1932–1958*. Edited by C. A. Meier, translated by David Roscoe. Princeton, New Jersey: Princeton University Press, 2001.

Karlsen, Barbara. *The Terrain Is Everything: An Ontology of Inter-species Becoming,* unpublished manuscript.

Kean, Leslie. *Surviving Death: A Journalist Investigates Evidence for an Afterlife*. New York: Crown Archetype, 2017.

Keppel, Anne-Marie. *Death Nesting: Ancient & Modern Death Doula Techniques, Mindfulness Practices and Herbal Care*. Rochester, Vt.: Inner Traditions, 2023.

Khenchen Palden Sherab Rinpoche and Khenpo Tswwang Dongyal Rinpoche. *Splendid Presence of the Great Guhyagarbha: Opening the Wisdom Door of the King of All Tantras*. Sidney Center, N.Y.: Dharma Samudra Prayer Books, 2011.

Kyger, Joanne. "Untitled." In *Ecology and Consciousness: Traditional Wisdom on the Environment*, edited by Richard Grossinger. Berkeley: North Atlantic Books, 1978.

Lafitte, Luke. *Machine Intelligence and the Imaginal Realm: Spiritual Freedom, and the Reanimation of Matter*. Rochester, Vt.: Inner Traditions, 2022.

Lash, John Lamb. *Not in His Image: Gnostic Vision, Sacred Ecology, and the Future of Belief.* White River Junction, Vt.: Chelsea Green Publishing, 2006.

Lawlor, Robert. *Voices of the First Day: Awakening in the Aboriginal Dreamtime.* Rochester, Vt.: Inner Traditions, 1991.

Lévi-Strauss, Claude. *The Raw and the Cooked: Introduction to a Science of Mythology,* vol. 1. Translated by John and Doreen Weightman. New York: Harper & Row, 1969.

Lewis-Kraus, Gideon. "How the Pentagon Started Taking UFOs Seriously." *New Yorker,* May 10, 2021.

Lindell, Jeffery A. "A Historical and Physiological Perspective of the Foo Fighters of World War Two." The Wayback Machine, 1991.

Loeb, Avi. *Extraterrestrial: The First Sign of Intelligent Life Beyond Earth.* New York: Houghton Mifflin Harcourt, 2021.

Lomax, John A. *Cowboy Songs and Other Frontier Ballads.* Lincoln, Nebraska: University of Nebraska Studies in Language, Literature, and Criticism, 1911.

Margulis, Lynn, and Dorian Sagan. *Origins of Sex.* New Haven: Yale University Press, 1990.

McFall, Caitlin. "Rubio Wants Answers on 'UFOs' Reported over US Military Posts." Fox News Online, May 23, 2021.

McKay, Matthew. *The Luminous Landscape of the Afterlife: Jordan's Message to the Living on What to Expect after Death.* Rochester, Vt.: Park Street Press, 2021.

McKenna, Terence. "Dreaming Awake at the End of Time." Sound Photosynthesis, San Francisco, December 13, 1998.

———. "The Last Interview, A Conversation with Erik Davis." Big Island, Hawaii, Soundcloud, November 1999.

Moaveni, Azadeh. *Guest House for Young Widows.* New York: Random House, 2019.

Olson, Charles. *Causal Mythology.* San Francisco: Four Seasons Foundation, 1969.

Overbye, Dennis. Review of Brian Greene, *Until the End of Time: Mind, Matter, and Our Search for Meaning in an Evolving Universe.* New York Review of Books, March 8, 2020.

Peake, Anthony. *Is There Life After Death: The Extraordinary Science of What Happens When We Die.* London: Arcturus Publishing Limited, 2012.

Peirce, Charles Sanders. *Collected Papers of Charles Sanders Peirce,* vol. 1. Edited by Charles Hartshorne and Paul Weiss. Cambridge, Mass.: Harvard University Press, 1931.

Plato. *The Apology of Socrates.* Translated by Benjamin Jowett. Portland, Maine: Thomas B. Mosher, 1910.

Ploum, Albrecht. *Spiegel van het Universum.* Landsgraaf, Netherlands: Hoppers Uitgeverijen, 1996. Informally translated by Hank Meldrum as *Mirrors of the Universe: The Cosmic Face of Earth—Shape Resemblances between Cosmic, Terrestrial, and Biological Structures.*

Rappaport, Roy. "Sanctity and Adaptation." In *Ecology and Consciousness: Traditional Wisdom on the Environment,* edited by Richard Grossinger. Berkeley: North Atlantic Books, 1992.

Roberts, Jane. *The Unknown Reality,* vol. 2. San Rafael, Calif.: Amber Allen Publishing, 1996.

Roth, Steve. "His Holiness the Sixteenth Karmapa at Hopi Mesa." Karma Triyana Dharmachakra. kagyu.org, 1974.

Sandburg, Carl. *Chicago Poems.* New York: Dover Publications, 2012.

Schwab, Sid. *Cutting Remarks: Insights and Recognitions of a Surgeon.* Berkeley: North Atlantic Books, 2006.

Scorsese, Martin, dir. *The Last Temptation of Christ.* Universal City, Calif.: Universal Pictures, 1988.

Shakespeare, William. *The Tempest,* 1610–1611. Published in 1623. *The Complete Works of William Shakespeare.* Garden City, New York: Doubleday & Company, 1936.

———. *The Tragedy of Hamlet, Prince of Denmark,* 1600. *The Complete Works of William Shakespeare.* Garden City, New York: Doubleday & Company, Inc., 1936.

———. *The Tragedy of Macbeth,* 1606. *The Complete Works of William Shakespeare.* Garden City, New York: Doubleday & Company, 1936.

Shyamalan, M. Night, dir. *The Sixth Sense*; Burbank, Calif.: Buena Vista Pictures, 1999.

Singer, Michael, J. *The Untethered Soul: The Journey beyond Yourself.* Oakland, Calif.: New Harbinger Publications, 2007.

Sogyal Rinpoche. *Dzogchen and Padmasambhava.* Berkeley, California: Rigpa Fellowship, 1990.

Spector, Brandon. "Frozen tardigrade becomes first 'quantum entangled' animal in history, researchers claim." LiveScience.com, December 20, 2021.

Stapledon, Olaf. *Star Maker.* London: Methuen and Company, 1937.

Steiner, Rudolf. *Cosmic Memory: Atlantis and Lemuria.* New York: HarperCollins, 1981.

Strieber, Whitley, and Anne Strieber. *The Afterlife Revolution*. San Antonio, Tex.: Walker and Collier, 2017.

Sturtevant, William C., and Alfonso Ortiz. *Handbook of North American Indians*, vol. 10: *Southwest*. Washington, D.C.: Smithsonian Institution, 1983.

Swain, Tony. *A Place for Strangers: Toward a History of Australian Aborigine Being*. Cambridge, UK: Cambridge University Press, 1996.

Swimme, Brian. *The Hidden Heart of the Cosmos: Humanity and the New Story*. Maryknoll, New York: Orbis Books, 1996.

———. *The Universe Story: From the Primordial Flaring Forth to the Ecozoic Era—A Celebration of the Unfolding of the Cosmos*. San Francisco, HarperOne, 1994.

Taylor, Victor E., and Charles E. Winquist. *Encyclopedia of Postmodernism*. London: Taylor & Francis, 2001.

Teilhard de Chardin, Pierre. *The Phenomenon of Man*. Translated by Bernard Wall. New York: Harper and Row, 1959.

Tsoknyi Rinpoche and Ngawang Gyatso. *Fearless Simplicity: The Dzogchen Way of Living Freely in a Complex World*. Boudhanath, Hong Kong, Esby: Ranjung Yeshe Publications, 2003.

Vachler, Petr, dir. *Top Secret UFO Projects: Declassified*. Netflix, 2021.

Vallée, Jacques. *Passport to Magonia: From Folklore to Flying Saucers*. Chicago: Henry Regnery and Company, 1969.

Wakefield, Stephanie. *Anthropocene Back Loop: Experimentation in Unsafe Operating Space (Critical Climate Chaos: Irreversibility)*. London: Open Humanities Press, 2020.

Weinberg, Steve. *The First Three Minutes: A Modern View of the Origin of the Universe*. New York: Basic Books, 1977.

Weir, Peter. *The Last Wave*. Beverly Hills, Calif.: United Artists, 1977.

Wheelwright, Philip, ed. *The Presocratics*. Indianapolis, Ind.: Odyssey Press, 1966.

Whitney, Alexandra. *Map of the Heart: An East-West Understanding of Heart Intelligence*. Unpublished thesis, California Institute of Integral Studies.

Wilder, Thornton. *The Bridge of San Luis Rey*. New York: Albert & Charles Boni, 1928.

Williams, William Carlos. *Journey to Love*. New York: Random House, 1955.

Index

ABOUT THE AUTHOR

Robert Morris is the senior pastor of Gateway Church, a multi-campus church based in the Dallas-Fort Worth Metroplex. Since it began in 2000, the church has grown to more than 100,000 active attendees. His television program airs in over 190 countries, and his radio program, *Worship & the Word with Pastor Robert*, airs in more than 6,400 cities. He serves as chancellor of The King's University and is the bestselling author of numerous books, including *The Blessed Life*, *Frequency*, *Beyond Blessed*, and *The God I Never Knew*. Robert and his wife, Debbie, have been married forty-three years and are blessed with one married daughter, two married sons, and nine grandchildren.